Unmasking DEI

EMERALD CRITICAL STUDIES IN INCLUSION, PRACTICE, AND IMPACT

Series Editors: Paul Ian Campbell

Emerald Critical Studies in Inclusion, Practice, and Impact fills the current lacuna of research informed and evaluated guidance in relation to inclusion in areas such as education, industry and communities, by providing a collection of critical case studies which provides new critical insights into equity and inequity. Importantly, the books provide a repository for case studies which provide explicit guidance for leaders, practitioners and policymakers interested in making their own sectors and practice more inclusive. In particular, *Emerald Critical Studies in Inclusion, Practice, and Impact* opens critical, theoretical and empirically informed debate around effective and measurable frameworks for change, what change in contemporary practices look like and how to better ensure inclusion works equitably and for the target audience.

Published Title

The Undeserving Polish Migrants: Homeless in a Place Called Home
by Magdalena Brzeska

Unmasking DEI: New Frameworks for Confronting Anti-Black Racism in the Black Atlantic

BY

CHRISTOPHER STUART TAYLOR

Associate Vice-President of Equity, Diversity, Inclusion, and Anti-Racism (The University of Waterloo), Canada

emerald PUBLISHING

United Kingdom – North America – Japan – India – Malaysia – China

Emerald Publishing Limited
Emerald Publishing, Floor 5, Northspring, 21–23 Wellington Street, Leeds LS1 4DL

First edition 2026

British Library Cataloguing in Publication Data
A catalogue record for this book is available from the British Library

ISBN: 978-1-83708-359-6 (Print)
ISBN: 978-1-83708-356-5 (Online)
ISBN: 978-1-83708-358-9 (Epub)

INVESTOR IN PEOPLE

Contents

About the Author

Christopher Stuart Taylor is the Associate Vice-President of Equity, Diversity, Inclusion & Anti-Racism (EDI-R) at the University of Waterloo. He is also an Associate Professor in the Department of History. He completed his PhD at Western University (Canada) in History and Migration & Ethnic Relations (MER). His first book, *Flying Fish in the Great White North: The Autonomous Migration of Black Barbadians*, is available from Fernwood Publishing. He also worked in the Ontario Public Service (OPS) and began his career as a Policy Coordinator Intern in the Deputy Minister's Office at the Ministry of Labour. He was the Diversity and Inclusion Coordinator in the Ministry of the Attorney General's Diversity, Inclusion & Accessibility Office; a Senior Policy Advisor at Ontario's Anti-Racism Directorate; and Manager of Social Justice & Change Cluster at the Ontario Correctional Services College. Dr Taylor is a proud founding member of the University of Waterloo's Black Faculty Collective (BFC).

Chapter 1

Introduction

I will admit, I would not have predicted that my career, and in many ways my life, would be shaped by the roller coaster that is diversity, equity and inclusion (DEI – in Canada and the United Kingdom, it may be more commonly known as 'EDI'). I was a DEI professional, a DEI scholar, a DEI consultant, and the post-25 May 2020 anti-thesis of merit: a DEI-hire. Who would have thought that the Black son of Barbadian (Bajan) newcomers, 'Black Brits' born in the mid-20th-century British colony of Barbados, would become the bane of the existence of some of the most powerful people in the world? That my very existence, scholarship and profession would become the lightning rod for an alt-right backlash of all things DEI and 'woke'?

I mean, ultimately, they may have thought that would be the case because I am Black in a fundamentally anti-Black society. A society that is shaped by the exclusion and dehumanization of people of darker skin tones; the ones that we love when they sing and dance, or kick a ball or score a goal, but loath to the core of its modern existence if they sit next to you at a lunch counter, on a bus or in a boardroom. My Blackness, my existence, my Self, has been deemed unworthy. It rests in the confines of spectacle or disdain. To be discarded or parroted. To be mocked or killed.

I say that not as hyperbole. I do not say it as a joke or to make anyone feel bad about themselves, or what their parents or ancestors did or didn't do. I say this as context for us to feel the words that I present to you in this book. Yes, feel. Not just read, but also feel. Before anyone reads this book, I want you to pause and think about where you were and what you were doing on 25 May 2020. I will start.

The Year the World Went Quiet: 2020

For me to remember 25 May 2020, I need to go back to February 2020. As a part of my upper-year course at the University of Waterloo, Canada, titled 'The

Unmasking DEI, 1–11

doi:10.1108/978-1-83708-356-520261001

Black Atlantic', I had organized a trip to Ghana with students and members of broader communities around the region. I even brought my Mother along as it was her first trip to the Continent. The experiential learning was a success. With a mixed group of Black, White and Brown participants, we travelled and let tears flow in the dungeons of the enslaved in the Cape Coast Castle. We shared laughs and anxious thoughts on bus trips to experience the Last Bath of enslaved ancestors, followed by our travels by road to Kumasi. We disagreed, we challenged each other's 'racial' and national identities in the cauldron that is interpersonal race relations under the stress of travel, time zone changes, and upset stomachs. We did it all, and we learnt. We created *communitas*, a community brought together by a shared experience. Who would have thought that this trip would foreshadow what was to be an avalanche of 'talking circles' that was to come my way for the rest of the calendar year?

Before we left in February 2020, there were whispers (some louder than others) about this mysterious illness. It was not anything that particularly worried any of us on the trip, as no one cancelled after months of planning. We did not wear masks on the plane ride, and any cough or chill we assumed was simply from travel and exhaustion. Little did we know that this would be the last bit of international travel for all of us for the rest of 2020, and for many, well into 2022 and beyond.

My last class of 'The Black Atlantic' was in March 2020. It was the Thursday before March Break, which is a weeklong spring break for elementary and secondary school students in Canada. Rumours had been swirling that there that schools may shut for a couple of weeks to get this virus under control. Needless to say, one week turned into one month, which in turn became one year (and counting) of Work From Home (WFH) life.

Do you remember the global shutdowns? Do you remember the isolation? Do you remember the deaths in long-term care homes? Do you remember the hospitals around the world on the brink of collapse? Do you remember the fear of neighbours, strangers and anyone who did not live in your household? I know I remember during that first week or so; a very odd, but familiar feeling. I remember that this 'threat of the Other' was not new to me. I remember feeling an odd, and almost perverse, sense of peace. I thought to myself: 'Wow, now the world knows what it likes to be me, a Black man, seen as a physical threat by just existing'. The world was Black. In more ways than one.

This context is important to situate why 25 May 2020 had such a superficial impact. We, as a global society, seem to have the collective memory of a goldfish when considering how devastating the pandemic was to our lives, livelihoods and ways of being. If we were to talk about 'system change' and how long it takes systems, particularly government systems, to change, we would be living in the upside-down in a matter of weeks. In the spring and summer of 2020, in many places around the world, we could not congregate in groups outside. In many parts of Canada, children could not play outside on playgrounds or sport fields. You could be fined or detained for exercising. However, there is one thing that we, in Canada, and across many countries could do to circumvent these by-laws: fall back on our Charter Rights and our freedom for peaceful assembly

(Government of Canada, 2024, Sec. 2.c). Yes, it was our fundamental right to come together – in groups of three or more – to gather, protest, and express our collective grievances about the topic *de jour*. This, I believe, was the perfect storm of cabin fever, social isolation and the unfortunate vicarious trauma of Darnella Frazier's recording of the murder of George Floyd on 25 May 2020.

Were people angry? Yes, but not as angry to create lasting change. They just wanted out of the house, and this was a convenient excuse. I am not saying this to diminish the real and valued pain that many felt, that I felt, when the realities of our collective Black mortality were on timeline after timeline, as the protagonist of millions of 2020 doomsday scrolls. I am providing this context to situate this book, unmask DEI, and tell the why DEI was never really about change, nor about supporting systemic change for Black people on a broader scale. It was a moment of time when all eyes – the only eyes – in the world were fixated on Black lives for 8 minutes and 46 seconds. A period of time when our dehumanization rose to the public consciousness.

Let's face it; the West, particularly the United States, had some of the highest rates of COVID-19 infections and related deaths in the world. A little bit of anti-Black racism and police brutality, rooted in the fabric of the United States' constitution and *raison d'être*, was a casual distraction to a silent killer that the country had no desire to contain. I can see the conversations in boardrooms across the West; 'If we give them some piecemeal and superficial concessions to support Black, Indigenous, and People of Colour (BIPOC) and "diverse" people, under the guise of confronting anti-Black racism, maybe they will ignore how poorly we handled this pandemic. If we also put a couple of Black people in contract senior positions in our company, throw in a VP or a C-suiter for good measure, maybe it will seem like we "fixed" racism? Brilliant idea'.

If we all had this understanding in 2020, the backlash 5 years later would not have come as a surprise. The shift from confronting anti-Black racism in May and June, to focusing on BIPOC communities, to it all getting subsumed and subsequently thrown away as DEI, would make perfect sense. I think that this was never supposed to work. This was designed to fail. DEI for Black people was always the ruse to appease and please. This is where the 2020 story started, but the failure of DEI was decades, *centuries* in the making.

In the tapestry of my history, the threads of my ancestors' stories are woven with resilience, perseverance, and an enduring quest for justice. Our journey begins with William Pitt, a figure enshrined in the annals of enslavement. The one person that I have been able to trace back to my maternal side to enslavement. Without being able to locate birth records, we assume he was born in Barbados, a land both beautiful and scarred, and endured the brutality of an inhumane system. William's story is not just a tale of survival but a testament to the indomitable spirit of the enslaved. As he toiled under the merciless sun, a sun that tourists now seek for relaxation and holiday, the promise of freedom lingered on the horizon like an elusive mirage. In Barbados, the echoes of Emancipation reverberated through the island, but true equity remained a distant dream. As my Father moved to Brixton, in the United Kingdom as a part of the mistreated Windrush Generation – the post-War cohort of young West Indians that helped 'rebuild' the United Kingdom but faced, and face, ongoing anti-Black racism. My Mother moved to Canada and worked as a teacher and eventually became one of the first – and few – Black woman principals in the city of Toronto. Needless to say, the kind of anti-Black racism they faced as post-War Black colonial 'pioneers' was the kind of oppression I could only imagine in the 2010s and 2020s as I was building my career. It is a brutal, unspoken truth – a deep wound of racism that many from that generation cannot voice, because the pain is unbearable. They both encountered a society grappling with the vestiges of colonialism and racism. The promises of DEI initiatives often rang hollow, as the systems in place failed to uplift those they were meant to serve by design. While contested, I use the term 'West Indian' to address the colonial oppression of African Caribbean peoples of former British colonies in the Caribbean.

Our journey did not end there. As we made our way to Canada, the land of supposed multiculturalism, we faced a new set of challenges. The rhetoric of DEI often masks the underlying systemic issues. The policies and initiatives were commendable in theory but fell short in practice, leaving my family and many others in a perpetual struggle for genuine recognition and fair treatment.

In each chapter of our history, Black people (in this book, I define this group – my group – as being someone of Sub-Saharan African Descent) have been instrumental in shaping the societies we inhabit, yet we have repeatedly found ourselves marginalized and disregarded. Our family's narrative is a reflection of the broader Black experience – a continuous fight for equality, dignity, and respect.

*Post*racism and My Relationship to DEI

As you flip through the pages of this book, you will notice that I have a complicated and at times contradictory relationship with DEI. I live and work in the space of what scholar Paul Campbell (2024) has termed *post*racism: 'a reference to a space where all or any manifestations of racial discriminations and anti-racism seamlessly and simultaneously co-exist, despite their apparently antithetical relationship' (p. 147). As it relates to Predominantly White Institutions (PWIs), Campbell (2024) identifies '*post*racial' spaces as,

> a space where people or a person of colour can be simultaneously hired, promoted, celebrated and supported alongside experiencing race-based structural inequalities, microaggressions and psychological violence – and, even by the same policies, designed to open the space up to them, or by the very same people who claim to be their allies. (p. 148)

In essence, I am in the embodiment of this co-habitation and co-existence of two seemingly contradictory ideologies. Ideologies that, in fact, are co-dependent in their abilities to agitate and disappoint the Right and the Left.

On one hand, DEI is my livelihood; I ply my trade as a senior administrator in DEI and anti-racism in a globally recognized post-secondary institution. Prior to working in academia in Canada, I had bureaucratic roles at different levels of government. I am a sought-after speaker and consultant in the 'DEI' space, and I have published, researched, and taught on the subject for a number of years. I was doing this work well before the Negro-Apocalypse of 25 May 2020. Some have even told me that this is my vocation. To even take it a step further, the precursors to DEI in Canada – multiculturalism and liberalized immigration policies – are what have shaped my personal identity. As a child of Barbadian (Bajan) newcomers of the 1960s, I cannot ignore the fact that their status as Canadians would not have been possible without the official deracialization of Canadian immigration policy in 1962. I cannot ignore the fact that the reason they had the opportunities to create, fund, and support Barbadian-Canadian clubs and institutions, including the National Council of Barbadian Associations in Canada (NCBAC), was due to the 1971 policy and ideological push for multiculturalism and the hyphenated identity culture that Canada is known for. I cannot ignore the fact I was raised in Canada, in a Bajan household, with a profound Black Bajan-Canadian identity as a dual citizen, with a double-migration father of the Windrush Generation, a mother that came to this Canada due to a teaching shortage, because Canada's Charter of Rights and Freedoms allowed them and I to exist and flourish in this country as 'true' Canadians. I cannot ignore the fact that both of my graduate degrees have specializations in migration and ethnic relations, the academic reality of DEI before DEI. It would be unfair for me to sit in a position to say that DEI is not a fabric of my identity. However, people, like DEI, are complex.

On the other hand, throughout my time in this DEI world, I have consistently poked holes in its value, validity and valour for true systemic and institutional change. I also cannot ignore the fact that DEI's mainstream relevance came to be to subdue the calls to confront anti-Black racism after 25 May 2020. I also cannot ignore the fact that my role is a DEI senior administrator is an institutional carwash – what authors' Too Black and Rasul A. Mowatt (2024) refer to as 'laundering Black rage' – 'how the Rage directed at the police murder of George Floyd could be marshalled to funnel the Black Lives Matter movement into corporate advertising and questionable leadership, while increasing the police budgets inside the laundry cities of capital' (p. i). That my, a cishet able-bodied Black man, ostensible 'executive leadership' role is to keep away what Robert F. Williams (1962) describes as the 'Negroes With Guns'; the 'aggressive' BLM Black peoples that were no longer asking for change, but demanding it. I cannot ignore the fact that despite the official deracialization of Canadian immigration policy in 1962, the Points System in 1967, and more modern Canadian immigration policies, practices and procedures continue to discriminate against Black newcomers, particularly refugees and temporary foreign workers in the 2020s. I also cannot ignore the fact that Canada's multiculturalism policy was designed on the premise of assimilation (ahem, inclusion), where newcomers and the Other must fit within Canada's English/French bi-cultural framework.

In plain language, in order to *be* different, you still need to fit within dominant White hegemonic power structures. I also cannot ignore the fact that across the United States, the United Kingdom and Canada, Black men who look like me continue to be incarcerated at higher rates and murdered by the state. Whether by the hands of law enforcement or the unflinching commitment to the perpetuation of White moderate systems of justice, education, and child welfare. I live in a multiplicity of identities. You will notice this even in the words of this book: how I shift from academic prose grounded in historical and scholarly research, to scathing critiques of DEI with unabashed fervour for unapologetic and uncompromising change. I live in the margins of a unique position of being the 'outside-insider.' I have the insider's privileged knowledge of systems, but the outsider's desire to deconstruct and dismantle. It is a fine balance. Why? As the insider, I am compensated for 'playing the game,' a position that most outsiders cannot, or do not, benefit. It is a position that I have learnt to make peace with, but it is not one I take for granted. The objective of this book is to trace the challenges of DEI and my identities; however, it will ultimately situate that for all its mainstream champions and detractors, DEI has been, and will always be, a tool of the state to control Black and other non-White people. To achieve this objective, the book is structured as follows:

Chapter 2: DEI Explained

This chapter critically examines the frameworks of DEI, arguing that mainstream DEI practices often serve as superficial solutions that fail to address systemic inequalities. It introduces the concept of *appeasement DEI*, a concept I define as referring to the institutional performative approach to DEI that prioritizes optics over structural change. Through historical and international comparisons (Canada, UK, US), the chapter explores how DEI has evolved from civil rights movements and multicultural policies, often reinforcing existing power structures. In this chapter, I reflect on my own complex relationship with DEI, acknowledging both the opportunities it has provided and the contradictions it embodies, particularly in the wake of George Floyd's murder. Ultimately, the chapter calls for a radical reimagining of DEI that centres justice, accountability and transformation.

Chapter 3: A History of Blackness and DEI

This chapter traces the historical construction of Blackness and its entanglement with systems of oppression, from biblical misinterpretations like the Curse of Ham to the rise of race science and colonial capitalism. It argues that DEI frameworks are rooted in centuries-old ideologies that dehumanized Black people to justify enslavement and economic exploitation. Drawing on scholars like Olaudah Equiano, Paul Gilroy, and Eric Williams, the chapter situates DEI within a legacy of racialized labour control and colonial appeasement. It critiques DEI as a modern extension of these systems, offering symbolic inclusion without dismantling institutional power. The chapter also highlights the Canadian context, using figures like Burnley 'Rocky' Jones to illustrate how racism continues to operate in Canada, subtly but pervasively. It concludes by asserting that DEI must be understood through the lenses of power, class and historical continuity – not just race.

Chapter 4: The Negro-Apocalypse

This chapter introduces the concept of the *Negro-Apocalypse* to describe the post-2020 racial reckoning sparked by George Floyd's murder. It situates this moment within a long history of Black resistance – from Tacky's War to the Rodney King riots – and argues that the backlash against DEI is rooted in White fear of losing identity and power. Drawing on thinkers like James Baldwin and Paulo Freire, the chapter critiques DEI as a tool of appeasement that pacifies Black rage while preserving White supremacy. It explores how DEI initiatives often force Black leaders to conform to White institutional norms, creating a façade of progress. The chapter also examines Canada's role in global anti-Blackness, highlighting how policies like multiculturalism and the International Decade for People of African Descent have failed to address systemic racism. Ultimately, the chapter warns that without confronting the roots of anti-Blackness, DEI will remain a mechanism of control rather than liberation.

Chapter 5: DEI, Anti-Black Racism and the University's Response to the Negro-Apocalypse

This chapter explores how PWIs, particularly universities, responded to the racial reckoning following the murder of George Floyd that catalyzed the Negro-Apocalypse. It critiques the superficial adoption of DEI frameworks that often reinforce White supremacy rather than dismantle it. Drawing on scholars like Frances Lee Ansley, Tema Okun, and Frantz Fanon, the chapter dissects how White supremacy manifests in institutional behaviours and governance. It critically examines the Scarborough Charter, a Canadian initiative aimed at addressing anti-Black racism in higher education, arguing that while well-intentioned, it too risks reinforcing elitist and assimilationist ideals under the guise of *Black Excellence*. The chapter also introduces the concept of the *racial conduit* – a framework for non-Black allies to use their power responsibly – and calls for reparations, radical accountability, and a reimagining of justice beyond performative DEI.

Chapter 6: The Silent Years – Black Presence at the University of Waterloo, 1960s–1970s

This chapter offers a historical case study of Black presence and exclusion at the University of Waterloo (UW) from its founding in the 1950s through the 1970s. It reveals how Black students and faculty were largely absent from institutional narratives, despite their contributions and presence. The chapter traces the university's Cold War-era origins, emphasizing its focus on technical education and co-operative learning on a global scale, while highlighting how Black international students – particularly from Africa and the Caribbean – were welcomed only as temporary 'development targets'. It documents the decline in Black faculty hiring post-1970s, attributing it to shifting immigration policies, racialized labour fears, and the fallout from events like the Sir George Williams Affair. The 'Silent Years' refers to the decades-long erasure of Black academic presence, despite earlier contributions by pioneering Black faculty. The chapter concludes by questioning whether UW, and similar institutions, can rise to meet today's social justice challenges as they once did for Cold War imperatives. Credit to one of my research assistants, Jonathan Chan, for his work in developing this chapter.

Chapter 7: New Ways Forward – Black-First *Praxis*

This chapter ushers in Part II of the book – the action-oriented Black-focused models for change. It ties together the concept of the 'Negro-Apocalypse' as a post-2020 racial reckoning with the critiques of the failure of DEI frameworks. The chapter restates that DEI, while well-intentioned, is ultimately a system-preserving mechanism that cannot deliver true Black liberation with its prioritization of assimilation into oppressive systems. This chapter explores cultural and theoretical frameworks for Black liberation through soca music and Afrofuturism. It argues that soca, like reggae, is a form of everyday resistance and a celebration of Black identity. Afrofuturism is presented as a tool for reimagining Black futures by blending history, science fiction, and cultural pride. Drawing on thinkers like Frantz Fanon and Eric Williams, the chapter explores how systemic racism adapts over time, masking oppression as progress. It calls for a return to ancestral knowledge, historical resistance and a redefinition of liberation that centres *Black-first praxis* – strategies rooted in Black history, culture and resistance.

Chapter 8: Barbados as a Model for Liberation

This chapter uses Barbados as a case study to explore Black resistance and liberation. It highlights key historical events such as the 1816 Bussa Rebellion and the 1937 People's Uprising, emphasizing the role of figures like Nanny Grigg and Clement Payne. The chapter critiques the sanitized narrative of Barbados as 'Little England' and instead positions it as a foundational site of Black resistance. It also examines the role of education in reinforcing colonial ideologies and introduces the concept of *edutocracy*, a fusion of education and plantocracy, which can explain how seemingly benevolent and progressive systems can perpetuate oppression and assimilation. The chapter concludes by challenging the reader to reconsider the compatibility of Western democratic ideals with true Black emancipation.

Chapter 9: Emancipatory Violence

This chapter shifts the conversation to a discussion of violence – not as physical aggression, but as a necessary response to systemic and epistemic violence. Drawing on Frantz Fanon, Nelson Mandela and Fred Hampton, it critiques the 'santaclausification' of Black revolutionaries and calls for a more radical, historically grounded approach to liberation. It ends by proposing guerrilla warfare and ideological resistance as viable strategies for confronting anti-Black racism in the 21st century.

Chapter 10: Conclusion: Reframing DEI and Owning Your Racism

The conclusion provides 'next steps' on how we can all reframe our thinking on what DEI means in our spheres of influence. How can we understand our *Self* as an inclusive leader that is willing to do the hard internal work to move the needle towards much more equitable institutions and, ultimately, societies? The conclusion provides detailed 'policy shorts' on actionable strategies and frameworks to 'reframe' DEI.

Concluding Comments: Jordans, Hoodies and Gold: Me, Myself and I

For me, one of the simplest ways of looking at this book, my *post*racial challenges of DEI, and my Blackness is *the hoodie versus the suit*. The hoodie really came into the public consciousness with the 2012 anti-Black murder of Trayvon Martin. It was the idea that a 'hooded' Black boy/youth/man was a threat to the lives of others. In my day-to-day, especially in my role as a senior administrator in one of Canada's top, globally recognized universities, my insistence (resistance/refusal?) to not conform to the wear-a-suit-and-tie mantra of a bureaucratic executive became the not-so-subtle awakening of anti-Blackness masking as the I in DEI – inclusion. In Matthew R. Morris' (2024) *Black Boys Like Me: Confrontations with Race, Identity, and Belonging*, he reflects on how his choice of wardrobe dictates how people saw his ability, competency and capacity to do his job as an educator. He wrote, 'Yet, the closer I got to being comfortable in my clothes, the further I fell from being considered "professional" in this "casual" environment' (p. 33). Clothes, to him and me, are a reflection of one's 'authentic' self and the environment that one lives, works and exists in. Morris (2024) further writes:

> The closer I got to being comfortable in my skin, the more often my button-downs were replaced by T-shirts. The closer I came to feeling safe in knowing that I was a Black man, the more often my gold chains would lay outside my shirt, not inside. (p. 33)

Unless you are on a sports team in post-secondary education, there is no uniform for students or professors for that matter. I have seen students roll out of bed and come to class in their pyjamas; I have seen professors roll out of bed and come to class in their pyjamas. I have seen professors wear (bike) shorts to department meetings, and senators and governors wear hiking boots and tattered t-shirts to decide on tuition increases and tenure files. There is a grey zone of 'professional' and 'casual' when it comes to university space. I came from the 9-5 corporate world where 'business casual' was the bare minimum. I used to work with lawyers and adopted the 'suit and tie' mantra; I have a closet full of suits, many of them bespoke and custom designed. If it is not a Double Windsor knot, I believe you might as well wear a clip-on tie. I would judge people (men) if the belt did not match the shoes, or if the socks did not match the outfit (unless it was a deliberate 'loud' print). Yes, I know how to dress, 'professionally.'

However, I also recognize that this idea of 'professional,' similar to this idea of the 'I' in DEI, inclusion, is about assimilation and conformity. It is about trying to make people fit into a dominant way of dress and a dominant way of being. It is the idea that the 'suit makes the man,' where that suit represents colonial conformity. In other words, if you need a suit to be included and seen as 'professional,' you must then assimilate into the dominant ways of being in academia. As a Black person, especially a Black man like myself, that means I cannot, and should not, wear the $400 Jordans, the (form-fitting) jeans that sit meticulously over those Jordans, and the custom hoodies made of premium cotton and cotton blends. In the warmer months, it means I must keep those tattoos covered and not wear a golf shirt, even if that is the standard 'business' dress when it is over 30 degrees centigrade. It means that my buttocks-length dreads would have to go, and the beard would need to be shorn. The diamond studs, pinky rings and three gold chains were removed. To be included means I would have to be less of myself. But is this not completely the opposite of what we/I am trying to represent, not only to my (authentic) Self, but more importantly, the tens of thousands of 17–25 year olds that want to see themselves in the people that run their universities and dictate their futures? How can we say DEI is working if we expect the 'DEI' boss to dress the same and follow Robert's Rules of Order? Would it not support the mental well-being of students of all shapes, sizes and colours to see administration at least be reflective of the student body in dress, word and deed? We expect post-secondary students to think critically, so why are we not critical of who is allowed to enter spaces in their own 'dress' (such as the White man full professors in shorts and sandals versus young Black assistant profs in Jordans and hoodies)?

When I was hired in this role as Associate Vice President (AVP), my boss, the Provost, asked me if I was going to start wearing suits. Guess what my response was? An emphatic 'no.'

This book begins not with theory, but with lived experience – mine. The Ghana field trip, the eerie silence of the pandemic and the global spectacle of Black death were not just moments; they were mirrors. They reflected the contradictions of DEI: its promises, its betrayals and its performative nature. These stories are not tangents. They are the foundation. They are the reason I can speak to DEI not just as a scholar or administrator, but as someone who has lived its contradictions. The chapters that follow are not just academic critiques, but excavations. They dig into the roots of DEI, its colonial scaffolding, its neoliberal polish and its anti-Black undercurrents. This introduction is the connective tissue between the personal and the political, between the narrative and the structure. It sets the stage for a central argument: DEI was never designed to liberate Black people. It was designed to contain us. And this book is my refusal to be contained.

This is the story of Unmasking DEI.

References

Campbell, P. I. (2024). *Race and assessment in higher education: From conceptualising barriers to making measurable change*. Emerald Publishing.

Government of Canada. (2024, December 1). Section 2(c) – Freedom of peaceful assembly. In *The Canadian charter of rights and freedoms*. https://www.justice.gc.ca/eng/csj-sjc/rfc-dlc/ccrf-ccdl/check/art2c.html

Morris, M. R. (2024). *Black boys like me: Confrontations with race, identity, and belonging*. Penguin Canada.

Too, B., & Mowatt, R. A. (2024). *Laundering Black rage: The washing of Black death, people, property, and profits*. Routledge.

Williams, R. F. (1962). *Negroes with guns*. Marzani & Munsell.

Part I

Unmasking DEI

Chapter 2

DEI Explained

DEI Explained

Diversity, equity, and inclusion (DEI) are often presented as progressive frameworks for organisational transformation. For me, DEI has been used as a tool to capitalise on human differences (which, in most organisations, equate to race or gender), to force those who are different to assimilate ('inclusion') within inequitable systems. As I argue in this book, these concepts are frequently deployed without addressing the historical and systemic roots of inequality they claim to dismantle. DEI in its popular form tends to focus on representation – who is in the room – without interrogating the structures that determine who gets to speak, who is heard, and who remains marginalised (Tessema et al., 2023). I argue that diversity is more than a demographic checklist; it must be understood in relation to power. Simply having a range of identities in a workplace does not guarantee justice. Equity, then, must go beyond equal access (Tessema et al., 2023) to include a reckoning with how systems have historically advantaged some while excluding others. Inclusion, too, must be more than a feeling; it must be a structural commitment to belonging, where marginalised voices are not only welcomed but centred (Tessema et al., 2023).

Establishing the 'E' in DEI

Equality (a term that people often confuse and conflate with 'equity') as Devine et al. (2022) note, is a contested terrain. While the UN Declaration of Human Rights proclaims universal dignity, the lived reality is that equality is often mediated through group-based struggles for recognition and justice (Devine et al., 2022). DEI initiatives that fail to acknowledge this complexity risk reproducing the very inequalities they seek to address. Indeed, implementation matters. As Iyer (2022) points out, when DEI is reduced to policy statements without meaningful engagement, it becomes performative, wasting resources and

Unmasking DEI, 15–35

doi:10.1108/978-1-83708-356-520261002

deepening intergroup tensions. As a colleague of mine once told me, this performativity carries 'social capital that universities use to market themselves' to 'sell' their product to donors, research funders, and key stakeholders: students and their parents. Those in positions of power – often members of historically advantaged groups, the power-*full* – must be held accountable for driving real change (Iyer, 2022). Meanwhile, those who are power-*less* face continued marginalisation in the meat-grinder that is the academic industrial complex. Finally, as Wolbring and Nguyen (2023) emphasise, institutions must recognise, and not misinterpret, intersectionality – the ways in which race, gender, class, and sexuality intersect to shape experiences of oppression. The term intersectionality, originally introduced by Kimberlé Crenshaw (1989), akin to other 'DEI' terminology, has been co-opted to entrench hegemonic domination of Whiteness for the power-*full,* under the guise of 'progress.' They can do this without having to acknowledge their own power positions, oppress others, and claim victimhood. Without this lens, DEI becomes a hollow gesture. True inclusion demands a radical reimagining of organisational culture, one that centres justice, accountability, and the full humanity of those most often excluded.

This all being said by respected scholars and practitioners, I argue that we need to have a much more nuanced understanding of DEI, particularly in 'multicultural' spaces such as Canada. Understanding Diversity, Equity, and Inclusion (DEI) requires a nuanced approach that goes beyond surface-level interpretations. Diversity is often misunderstood as merely racial representation. However, it encompasses a broader spectrum, including the 17 protected grounds under the *Human Rights Code* (1990), such as age, gender, disability, and more. This means that diversity is not limited to visible characteristics, but rather includes a wide range of human differences. Recognising diversity means acknowledging that everyone in society brings unique perspectives and experiences. This broad understanding helps in creating more inclusive environments where all forms of diversity are valued.

In my experience, equity is frequently mistaken for equal opportunity. However, equity is about fairness and justice, which involves providing more resources and support to those who need it most, similar to the principles of a progressive tax system in Canada. Implementing equity requires an understanding of systemic inequalities and addressing them by redistributing resources to level the playing field. This approach ensures that individuals who face greater barriers receive the necessary support to achieve similar outcomes as those with fewer obstacles.

Inclusion as a Means to Assimilation

Inclusion, the primary sticking point in the DEI debate, is often seen as making superficial changes to systems to accommodate diverse individuals. The challenge with inclusion lies in the misconception that it is about fitting diverse individuals into existing structures. However, true inclusion demands a deeper transformation of existing inequitable systems to integrate diverse perspectives and experiences at their core, creating environments where all individuals can thrive. Inclusion, therefore, should focus on reshaping these structures to be more equitable and inclusive. This approach requires a shift in mindset and practices to genuinely embrace and value differences.

By recognising the broader scope of diversity, the need for equitable resource distribution, and the transformative nature of inclusion, we can better address the complexities of creating truly inclusive and equitable environments. The challenge that most DEI practitioners face is that there is no such thing as 'one-size-fits-all' environment for creating an inclusive or equitable environment. However, the core and underlying principle is the humanisation of all bodies and creating space for them to reach their full (human) potential.

I argue that what we do at best in the West is what I call *appeasement DEI*; a form of DEI that makes surface-level changes (e.g. training sessions or hiring some non-White people in contract positions), but never really gets to the structural roots of the problem. Here, I challenged and commented on how some scholars and practitioners positioned *appeasement DEI*; the kind that is palatable to c-suiters and administrators, but is ultimately not very effective. As one former boss told me, this form of DEI is about cutting the crust off the bread, but you are still eating the same mouldy bread.

DEI in the UK

The Commonwealth Immigrants Act *and Anti-Black Racism as Foundation*

Anti-Black racism was the underlying factor of a large number of central and local government policy decisions made in the UK in the 20th century, underscoring the DEI's inefficiencies in supporting Black life. This reality, though clear throughout UK history through the murder of Black people like Stephen Lawrence, is often not talked about enough. Two key examples of anti-Black racism in the UK include the *Commonwealth Immigrants Act* and the Windrush Generation. There cannot be a conversation on DEI in the UK without engaging in these conversations (see Appendix A).

Britain's 1962 *Commonwealth Immigrants Act* tried to limit the number of non-White immigrants from former British colonies while still allowing people from other countries, like Ireland, to enter freely. Ceri Peach (1968) argued that British immigration policies were driven by politics, not economics. Along these lines, the *Act* was a response to the political and social tensions caused by the increase in non-White immigrants after World War II. The British public pressured the government to restrict its open immigration policy and opposed bringing in migrants from their colonies after the war. The *Act*, which took effect on 1 July 1962, introduced new immigration rules and penalties for deportation for Commonwealth citizens, except those born in the UK or holding UK passports.

The British Conservative government gave in to social pressure, which Peach (1968) argued was racially motivated. The purpose of the *Act* was to restrict, not just regulate, the movement of Commonwealth immigrants, especially from predominantly non-White countries. Gary P. Freeman (1987) supported this view, stating that British immigration policy in the 1960s ignored the country's need for workers and was designed to slow down the influx of non-Whites, influenced by public opinion. Comparing race relations in the US and the UK, Gordon K. Lewis (1990) noted that while the US made progress with civil rights, Britain passed laws making it harder for non-White immigrants to enter, undermining the idea of the Commonwealth as a family of nations.

The *Act* did not explicitly mention race, but by limiting the entry of non-White immigrants, it reflected and reinforced post-war British racial and class attitudes. Racial tensions in Britain led to violent attacks on Black people and their property in Nottingham and Notting Hill in the late 1950s, culminating in the racially motivated murder of Kelso Cochrane in 1959. Elyse Dodgson (1984) argued that Black immigrants received unfair negative publicity after these racist attacks, which swayed public opinion in favour of stricter immigration controls.

Exploring Labour and Racialisation Through the Experiences of Black West Indians

The relationship between race and class both opened and closed the door for Black West Indian labour in post-war Britain. Ken Pryce (1977) discussed how Black West Indian migrants were marginalised as a racialised and immigrant labour class. He argued that West Indian migration had a class character shaped by colonialism and underdevelopment, starting with the period of enslavement and continuing with neo-imperialistic relations between Britain and the West Indies. Black West Indians were a subordinate labour class in British society, concentrated in the most low-paying, dangerous, and precarious jobs and abandoned during recessions. Pryce (1977) noted that post-war affluence in Britain led to the upward mobility of British workers, who moved into skilled and valued positions, while Black West Indian labour filled de-skilled jobs left by White workers due to technical innovation. Educated and upwardly mobile Black West Indians faced the harsh realities of a racialised labour market.

Economically, Britain needed this Black immigrant labour to support its growing White middle class. It seemed illogical for the government to restrict this cheap labour pool. Racial discrimination swayed public opinion. As we see today across the Black Atlantic, in countries led by the White power-*full* anti-immigrant or racist policies are driven by a sense of (White) nationalism. A sense of nationalism that cuts off its nose to spite its face. In the past, and even today, societies benefited from cheap (non-White) labour pools doing jobs that British citizens no longer wanted. Pryce (1977) concluded that the employment of cheap Commonwealth labour ensured the growth of the British economy, as West Indians lowered labour costs and could be used to divide the workforce along racial lines.

British racial prejudice overshadowed the realities of their capitalist system, reliant on a racialised immigrant class. Limited social mobility due to racism led some Black West Indians to consider re-emigrating to Canada, the United States, or returning to the West Indies. Racist public opinion continued to influence government policy, leading to stricter immigration requirements. In a few years, from the welcome of the S.S. Empire Windrush in 1948 to the *Commonwealth Immigrants Act* in 1962, the Black presence in Britain became unwanted. Fears of exclusion spread throughout Barbados and the West Indies, leading to a significant decline in Barbadian emigration to the UK, directly attributed to the *Act* (Barbados Government, 1965). As Britain closed its doors to non-White emigration, it forced Canada to re-evaluate its ideological nation-building philosophy of 'White Canada' and open its doors to 'diversity' migrants, which in turn paved the way for 'DEI' and official multiculturalism. From my perspective, it was likely not a coincidence that in 1962, the year Britain's *Commonwealth Immigrants Act* came into effect, Canada officially de-racialised their immigration policy. I argue that British diplomacy coerced the liberalisation of Canadian immigration and forced the country into a state of 'formal' DEI. This process is an example of the ways that anti-Black racism has been used as a tool to 'integrate' and 'assimilate' unwanted British subjects.

Neoliberalism and DEI: Individualist Approaches to 'Equity' That Mask Systemic Inequality

The implications of these DEI arguments are multifaceted and significant for the UK and beyond. The shift from equality to diversity and inclusion may create an illusion of progress without addressing underlying issues, leading to a cycle of 'collective amnesia' that prevents real, lasting change. The findings suggest that multi-session DEI and anti-racism trainings are more effective than one-time sessions, indicating that organizations need to invest in comprehensive training programs rather than singular checkboxes on training records to see meaningful improvements (Wang et al., 2024). Understanding the different types of equality – basic, opportunity, and condition – can help shape more effective policies, with the focus on equality of opportunity in the UK highlighting the need for a balanced approach that also considers equality of condition. Basic equality assumes that all humans have equal worth and importance; equality of opportunity acknowledges that inequalities in society need to be balanced so everyone gets an 'equal chance'; and equality of condition focuses on changing structural, systemic, and economic power imbalances (Baker et al., 2004). Neoliberal policies emphasising individualism and personal responsibility, which are more and more common as guiding frameworks for our institutions, further mask structural inequalities, suggesting a fundamental need to rethink these policies to address systemic issues more effectively. Alongside neoliberalism, the persistence of racism in institutions like universities indicates that current DEI efforts are insufficient, necessitating more proactive and comprehensive measures to support racialised and Indigenous scholars. Achieving true equity requires moving away from neoliberal structures, recognising group differences, and implementing transparent policies. This involves collecting data, setting benchmarks, and challenging established norms in hiring, evaluation, and promotion to create a more inclusive academic environment. Overall, the argument calls for a deeper, more systemic approach to DEI that goes beyond surface-level changes and addresses the root causes of inequality.

DEI in the United States

Historical Foundations: The Early 20th Century Roots of DEI

Unbeknownst to influential decision makers in the United States in the 2020s, the journey towards diversity, equity, and inclusion (DEI) in the United States began approximately 100 years ago, with significant milestones marking its progress (see Appendix A). Initially, the mainstream workforce was predominantly White men, leaving women, People of Colour, immigrants, and other marginalised groups without equal protection (Tessema et al., 2023). The establishment of the Women's Bureau in 1920, just before the ratification of the 19th Amendment, was one of the first significant steps towards inclusion, documenting wage inequalities and allowing women to sit for the Civil Service exam (Tessema et al., 2023).

The desegregation of the US Armed Forces through Executive Orders 8802 and 9981 further advanced DEI by mandating equal treatment and opportunity regardless of race, colour, national origin, or religion (Tessema et al., 2023). The *Civil Rights Act* of 1964 was a landmark legislation that prohibited discrimination based on sex, race, colour, religion, and national origin, effectively ending Jim Crow laws (Tessema et al., 2023). Subsequent acts, such as the *Equal Pay Act* of 1963, the *Age Discrimination in Employment Act* of 1967, and the *Pregnancy Discrimination Act* of 1978, continued to build on these foundations by addressing specific forms of discrimination (Tessema et al., 2023).

Corporate DEI Evolution: From 'Tokenism' to 'Strategic Inclusion'

In the private sector, the 1970s saw Fortune 500 companies emphasising diversity in hiring to attract a broader talent pool (Tessema et al., 2023). The 1980s marked a shift where skill became more important than race, gender, or creed, creating more opportunities for marginalized groups and women (Tessema et al., 2023). By the 1990s and 2000s, companies recognised the business impact of a diverse workforce that mirrored their consumer base, leading to increased efforts in hiring, training, and retaining diverse employees (Tessema et al., 2023).

The 2010s brought a focus on diversity leadership, with Millennials entering the workforce with expectations of diversity at all levels of corporate America. This led to the development of employee resource groups (ERGs) to foster inclusive workplaces (Tessema et al., 2023). Companies that excelled in DEI listened to their employees and prioritised their needs, creating a dynamic and innovative workforce (Tessema et al., 2023).

DEI in Canada: The True North Strong and (Kind of) Free

The Myth of Canadian Exceptionalism

This framing, present in our anthem, leader speeches, and global marketing, has formed the basis of the Canadian Diversity, Equity, and Inclusion (EDI in Canada) movement, which positions Canada as fundamentally better than the United States, and divorced from its British colonial past (see Appendix A). This is highlighted in its 'better' treatment of non-White people, especially Black and Indigenous individuals. This belief, however, is historically inaccurate and overlooks the true roots of Canadian DEI policies, which are based on misinterpretations of Pierre Trudeau's idea of 'multiculturalism within a bilingual framework'. Canada has a long history of integration efforts based on assimilation, attempting to incorporate Indigenous Peoples, as well as Black and immigrant people, into the ostensibly White body politic, indeed the 'Great White North' (Mullings et al., 2016; Taylor, 2013). Canada was intended to be a melting pot of White Anglophone and Francophone settlers, not a mosaic of different cultures. The current opposition to DEI in Canada reflects the country's history of right-wing extremism.

Appeasement DEI: Canadian DEI as Performative and Assimilationist

Canada has a long history of using DEI as a way to appease non-White people with promises of safety and mobility while creating conflicts with those who feel their power is threatened. The conflict I refer to here is the power-*full* feeling that they are becoming power-*less* by creating seemingly fairer systems that in fact entrench power in the hands of the elites to make them *full*-er. The roots of what I call 'appeasement DEI' in Canada began with the *Treaty of Paris* in 1763 and the *Quebec Act* of 1774. The nation-building project of the 19th century used non-White bodies as temporary workers to build the country, while early twentieth-century pro-White immigration policies often restricted their ability to benefit from Canadian citizenship (Baines & Sharma, 2002). Modern DEI efforts started in 1962 with the de-racialisation of immigration policy, followed by the 1971 multiculturalism policy, the 1976 *Immigration Act*, the 1982 *Canadian Charter of Rights and Freedoms*, the 1984 *Abella Commission*, and other initiatives. These policies, despite their stated goals to enhance equity and increase inclusion rooted in post-war human and civil rights movements, have only served to maintain the status quo, often deepening systemic inequalities, undermining Indigenous sovereignty and maintaining colonial efforts, and foregrounding neoliberal ideas of merit and equal opportunity. The following section attends to these policies, ranging in implementation from the 1700s to the late 1900s, to illustrate the ways in which their language and practice are often antithetical to true inclusion.

The (White) Colonial Roots of DEI: The Quebec Act

The *Quebec Act* of 1774 might seem like an odd thing to fit within the confines of DEI. However, I think it is very important that we look to our histories and redefine how we think about 'race' and even the smallest aspects of diversity, equity, and inclusion to truly understand where we are and where we have come. We often think about DEI as a 'new thing' starting in 2020; however, why not include the *Acts of Union* in 1707 to create the 'inclusive' Kingdom of Great Britain? Remember, this was a period where the 166 square miles of Barbados, an English and now British colony, was the crown jewel of imperialism and the dehumanisation of Black bodies for profit. Or how about the Civil War in 1861 in the United States, where White men killed their relatives in order to maintain their 'equitable' stance in the face of federal aggression to enslave and oppress Black bodies? In Canada, the standalone 'multicultural' nation-state, there are rarely conversations around the *Quebec Act* and its foundations as a key component in 'race relations' in Canada. The relation between French and English settler colonial forces in Turtle Island (what we now know as Canada) has also formed the foundations for the core tenets of DEI in Canada. The country that is ostensibly *the* global champion of multiculturalism (DEI) simultaneously enables the ongoing oppression and denial of Indigenous sovereignty, the exclusion of non-White people, and the maintenance of privilege for White people and White structures.

So, what is the *Quebec Act*? The British took control of what we now know as Canada (British North America) in 1763 following the signing of the Treaty of Paris that ended the Seven Years' War (Library and Archives Canada, 2024; University of Ottawa, n.d.). The *Act* was implemented as:

> governing the 'Province of Quebec' significantly enlarged the colony's territory with the addition of the Indian Territory created in 1763, a region that covered the north of the province from Labrador to the Great Lakes area. The Quebec Act reestablished civil law (Section 8) and religious freedom (Sections 5 and 7) in Canada, but English law continued to apply for criminal matters. (University of Ottawa, n.d., para. 3)

What is commonly known to most, 'French Canadians were given the right – albeit ambiguously – to use French in professing their religion and in the courts (civil matters)' (University of Ottawa, n.d., para. 4). University of Ottawa Professor, Jean-François Lozier, quoted the 1767 writings of Lord Shelburne, the Secretary of State for the Colony; 'Barring a catastrophe, shocking to think of, this country must, to the end of time, be peopled by the Canadian race' (Simard-Côté, 2024, para. 19). Lozier went on to say, 'from 1767, Carleton concluded that the province of Quebec would be inhabited by the Canadian race, the Canadian people, until the end of time, unless an unlikely catastrophe occurred. This led to a compromise' (Simard-Côté, 2024, para. 20). There are two pieces to unpack here: the idea of 'compromise' and the 'Canadian race'. On the issue of compromise, Martin Pâquet, historian and anthropologist at Université Laval, stated that a lasting legacy of the 1774 *Act* was the 'fact that we can establish a compromise and that we have to maintain harmony at that time. The fact that the spirit of harmony, the spirit of compromise, was sustainable' (Simard-Côté, 2024, para. 42). This was created during a period of time where religious, national, and ethnic tensions dictated the day-to-day realities of many people, particularly through physical violence. Pâquet positioned the *Quebec Act* as a true testament to community building and highlighted how it established the founding ethos of the 'I' in DEI – inclusion. Quebec, a province that has yet to sign on to Canada's 1982 *Constitution Act* and is constantly in the throes of separatism debates, has arguably the most 'Canadian' roots in present-day DEI. Pâquet stated:

> It's a philosophic question...I would say that life in a democracy, we have to consider the essence of democracy. The essence of democracy is that our societies are plural and diverse. There are divisions between men and women. There are divisions between ages, divisions between ethnic origins, religious divisions and so on. So, with all of these intersections, how do we create a community? That is fundamental in politics. It's a dimension – this question – it was an issue in 1774, at the time of the Quebec Act. It is just as relevant today, in the contemporary world, at the beginning of the 21st century, when we have differences that are as important. Ethnic differences, among others. Of origin too, which means the arrival of new citizens who have to integrate within the political context. So, we have to consider this diversity. And that is why the Quebec Act is topical. (Simard-Côté, 2024, para. 52)

Through compromise, the *Quebec Act* created a community. Whether we want to argue if it was a 'real' or 'imagined' community, the Act's purpose had, and continues to have, lasting reverberations on DEI. The DEI framework of the *Act* created the following: diversity, through different linguistic and religious groups; equity, by creating provisions for them to keep their sense of Self in the face of a dominant majority; and inclusion, through laws that allowed for them to be 'equal' members of society and live as Canadians.

The problem that we have in 21st century Canada, as well as across the United States and the United Kingdom, is that we no longer have historical memories that different groups of White 'nations' were considered different 'races'. In fact, we as a present-day collective society do not see 'White' as a 'race,' and if we do, it is usually seen as a bad thing (e.g. neo-Nazi White nationalism). This is not a simple oversight. This deliberate White supremacist obfuscation aligns with DEI that seeks to mark difference or the 'Other' from the 'White' norm. With the *Quebec Act*, 'The oath of allegiance was altered to omit reference to the Protestant faith and freedom to practice Catholicism was granted. This lifted a series of restrictions previously imposed on Catholic

French Colonists' (UK Parliament, n.d., para. 1). With all the debates surrounding non-Protestant newcomers 'changing' the fabric of 'Canadian values', it is quite interesting to me that 250 years ago, someone had the 18th century DEI foresight to acknowledge that law should protect difference; that these Christian differences, ones that (White) people killed each other for on both sides of the Atlantic for centuries, should be recognized as diverse and equitable, and ones that should be inclusive to create what we now know as Canada. The *Quebec Act* should be seen as the founding framework for DEI in Canada, and the twenty-century *Multiculturalism Policy* should be its long awaited sequel, cementing its legacy.

Multiculturalism Policy, the **Multiculturalism Act,** *and Legal Frameworks*

Canada's 1971 *Multiculturalism Policy*, which later became the 1988 *Canadian Multiculturalism Act* (*CMA*), aims to recognise and promote the cultural and racial diversity of Canadian society, ensuring that all members can preserve, enhance, and share their cultural heritage. It acknowledges multiculturalism as a fundamental aspect of Canadian heritage and identity, providing a valuable resource for shaping the country's future. The policy promotes full and equitable participation of individuals and communities of all origins in all aspects of Canadian society, helping to eliminate barriers to participation. It recognises the contributions of communities with common origins and enhances their development, ensuring equal treatment and protection under the law while respecting and valuing diversity (CMA, 1988).

Further, the policy encourages social, cultural, economic, and political institutions to be respectful and inclusive of Canada's multicultural character, fostering understanding and creativity from diverse interactions. It also aims to preserve and enhance the use of languages other than English and French, while strengthening the status and use of the official languages of Canada, promoting multiculturalism in harmony with the national commitment to these languages (Berry, 2013).

Under this policy, federal institutions are required to ensure equal employment opportunities for all Canadians, promote policies that help individuals and communities contribute to Canada's evolution, and enhance understanding and respect for diversity. They must collect data to develop responsive policies, utilise the language skills and cultural understanding of all origins, and operate in a manner sensitive to Canada's multicultural reality. The Minister coordinates the implementation of the policy, supporting related programs and encouraging activities that reflect Canada's multicultural reality. The Minister also supports research, promotes exchanges among communities, assists businesses and organisations in ensuring full participation and respect for multiculturalism, and helps minority communities overcome discrimination. Additionally, the Minister can enter into agreements with provinces and foreign states to promote multiculturalism (CMA, 1988).

An advisory committee may be established by the Minister to provide advice on multiculturalism. Committee members are compensated and reimbursed for travel expenses, and the committee submits an annual report on its activities and the implementation of the policy. In theory, the policy aims to create an 'inclusive' and respectful society that values and benefits from its cultural diversity. The preamble of the *Multiculturalism Act* (CMA, 1988) clearly states:

> the Government of Canada recognises the diversity of Canadians as regards race, national or ethnic origin, colour and religion as a fundamental characteristic of Canadian society and is committed to a policy of multiculturalism designed to preserve and enhance the multicultural heritage of Canadians while working to achieve the equality of all Canadians in the economic, social, cultural and political life of Canada. (para. 8)

The *Act*, one never to be confused with mainstream (mis)understandings of DEI, openly writes in law that 'the Constitution of Canada recognises the importance of preserving and enhancing the multicultural heritage of Canadians' (CMA, 1988, para. 2). A law that promotes diversity, equity, and inclusion through rights that state that:

> the Constitution of Canada provides that every individual is equal before and under the law and has the right to the equal protection and benefit of the law without discrimination and that everyone has the freedom of conscience, religion, thought, belief, opinion, expression, peaceful assembly and association and guarantees those rights and freedoms equally to male and female persons. (CMA, 1988, para. 1)

As an anti-racism scholar, Debra Thompson (2025) wrote:

> to be frank, a lot of what we call DEI isn't voluntary – it's the law. The Supreme Court of Canada has consistently affirmed that the Charter of Rights and Freedoms guarantees substantive equality, underscoring that colour-blind approaches that treat all people exactly the same can produce inequality. (para. 26)

Accordingly, the 1982 *Canadian Charter of Rights and Freedoms* 'protects a number of rights and freedoms, including freedom of expression and the right to equality. It forms part of our Constitution – the highest law in all of Canada – and is one of our country's greatest accomplishments' (Government of Canada, 2025, para. 1).

Section 15 ('Equality Rights') of the *Charter* (Government of Canada, 1982) affirms that:

> The basic purpose of Section 15(2) is to shield ameliorative programs from the charge of "reverse discrimination". That is, Section 15(2) enables governments to combat discrimination through programs aimed at helping disadvantaged groups without fear of challenge under Section 15(1) by groups that do not share that disadvantage (Kapp, supra at paragraph 16). In addition, Section 15(2) enables governments to assist one disadvantaged group, or subset thereof, without being paralysed by the necessity to assist all, including others who may suffer similar or equal disadvantage (Cunningham, supra at paragraph 41). (Sec. 15.5. iii)

What most anti-DEI proponents in Canada also do not want to recognise is that this promotion of 'unfairness' of DEI programmes that are seemingly against 'merit' is not up for debate, regardless of whether that debate is practical or ideological. Section 15(2), under 'Affirmative action programs', states that:

> (2) Subsection (1) does not preclude any law, programme or activity that has as its object the amelioration of conditions of disadvantaged individuals or groups including those that are disadvantaged because of race, national or ethnic origin, colour, religion, sex, age or mental or physical disability. (Sec. 15.2)

Not to say that these issues are 'equal,' but imagine the absurdity if there was a large portion of the public that was in favour of questioning whether it was okay or not to enslave Black people, when the *Emancipation Act,* which came into effect on 1 August 1834, clearly says it is against the law? Think about that for a second. Maybe the real motive behind anti-DEI is to reverse the humanisation of non-White peoples, particularly Black people, one that Rinaldo Walcott (2021) reaffirms is that we (Black people) have yet to be truly emancipated from their dehumanisation as property. Maybe, stick with me for a second, the real motive behind anti-DEI is what Koritha Mitchell (2018) refers to as 'know-your-place-aggression.' That Black people, those that were legally 'free' in the 19th century, got a little too uppity in twenty-first, and the White power-*full* had to knock them back into place. We have historical examples of this with the rise of the KKK in the late 19th and early 20th century; Jim Crow and segregation; and racist socio-economic policies across the Black Atlantic in the Post-War period.

Indigenous Sovereignty and DEI: Multiculturalism as the Masking Agent for Racism

This reality is very sobering. It was during the mid-20th century that Canada began to see the confrontation of colonised peoples on the stolen land of Turtle Island, specifically of Black Barbadians and Indigenous peoples. Following the de-racialisation of Canadian immigration policy in 1962 and the introduction of the Points System in 1967, more Emigrant Ambassadors could emigrate from the Island to the Great White North. However, during this period of growth of People of Colour in this settler state and the introduction of the Multiculturalism Policy in 1971, the Canadian government effectively used the physical presence of colonial subjects to perpetuate the further colonisation of Indigenous peoples. The lateral violence of power-*less* groups fighting over White-dominated and scarce resources and blaming each other for it. We have seen such examples in Uganda, which, interestingly enough, in 1972 became a beacon for Ugandans of South Asian descent expelled by Idi Amin. The 1960s paradox of hypocrite came during a 'period of unprecedented economic growth and prosperity' in Canada, as Indigenous children 'who attended residential schools continued to be poorly housed, poorly fed, poorly clothed, and poorly educated' (Truth and Reconciliation Commission of Canada [TRC], 2015, p. 11). This was most apparent in 1969s 'Statement of the Government of Canada on Indian Policy', or better known as the 'White Paper' (Government of Canada, 1969).

The ostensibly benevolent rhetoric surrounding the White Paper was said to be drawn from an inclusive, multicultural framework rooted in the equity and belonging of Indigenous Peoples as Canadians. It was at this point in time that policy rhetoric, however, shifted from one of segregation and extinction to the integration and assimilation of Indigenous Peoples (TRC, 2015). This is a form of cultural extinction, which, in the words of some Indigenous and Black scholars, is deemed as part of spirit murder (Revilla, 2021). The proposed policy promised that 'if Indian people are to become full members of Canadian society they must be warmly welcomed by that society', and 'to be an Indian must be to be free – free to develop an Indian culture in an environment of legal, social and economic equality with other Canadians' (Government of Canada, 1969, p. 5). This mirrors the language of *Multiculturalism Act,* whose stated purpose was to 'promote the full and equitable participation of individuals and communities of all origins in the continuing evolution and shaping of all aspects of Canadian society and assist them in the elimination of any barrier to that participation' (CMA, 1988, Sec. 3.1.c). Mirroring the language of inclusion and effectively designating Indigenous Peoples in this country as special interest groups, thereby negating their constitutional and legal status, the White Paper argued that 'the treatment resulting from their different status has been often worse, sometimes equal and occasionally better than that accorded to their fellow citizens', and 'the discrimination which affects the poor Indian and non-Indian alike, when compounded with a legal status that sets the Indian apart, provides dangerously fertile ground for social and cultural discrimination' (Government of Canada, 1969, p. 5).

The Government's rhetorical confusion of the ideals of Canadian multiculturalism and its conflation with negative codifiers have created a stratified hierarchy of acceptance for newcomers, Black people, and all People of Colour. Stratification exists on all levels of society and is formed, in part, by socio-economic factors, but issues around class and generational status only mask the racist overtones associated with the hierarchy of acceptance in

Canadian society. Indeed, race is a fundamental organising principle of Canadian society. Blackness has represented, and continues to be represented, with negative responses, leading to negative outcomes for Black youth in many institutions in Canada, particularly in the education and justice sectors. These DEI initiatives often provide a façade of progress without addressing systemic inequities; rather, they were designed to maintain colonial power structures. Multiculturalism and DEI were meant to allow for visible differences and the appearance of inclusion, all while maintaining ideological Whiteness.

Academic Institutions and Neoliberalism

Many scholars have critically examined the concept of diversity, equity, and inclusion, and its unique implications in Canadian society. Walcott, in his 2019 essay titled 'The End of Diversity', argues that diversity, historically tied to Canada's policy of multiculturalism, has become outdated and ineffective in promoting genuine change and inclusion. Despite governmental shifts towards anti-racism and equity, the persistence of racism, particularly against Black people, undermines the goal of a truly inclusive society. Walcott (2019) critiques the false beliefs held by White people about societal progress, noting that the notion of equal access to a good life through diversity is a myth. He views multiculturalism as a post-World War II construct that perpetuates Canada's predominantly White identity, excluding Black people and maintaining global White privilege (Walcott, 2019).

Walcott (2019) connects the idea of value to economic systems and racial inequality, arguing that concepts like diversity, equity, anti-racism, and social justice are rooted in these systems. He believes that true Black freedom opposes capitalism and that current inclusion efforts are linked to the history of Black enslavement. To address this history and present, Walcott (2019) calls for a new approach that transcends the language of diversity, advocating for new ways of relating to each other and constantly updating the idea of justice to counter ongoing colonial influences.

Similarly, *The Equity Myth*, authored by Henry et al. (2017), explores how universities, often seen as bastions of liberal democracy and fairness, are actually key sites where racism is subtly perpetuated. The authors argue that this denial of racism equates to a denial of equity, particularly for non-White and Indigenous scholars who face exclusion and marginalisation in various institutional practices (Henry et al., 2017). The book highlights the gap between the promise of social justice in ostensibly progressive institutions and the reality for racialised and Indigenous scholars, noting that systemic exclusion occurs through academic canons and methodologies that marginalise certain knowledge and scholars (Henry et al., 2017).

Recent studies, including, but not limited to, *the Report of the University of Toronto Anti-Black Racism Task Force* (Anti-Black Racism Task Force, 2021); *Understanding student perspectives: Racism, discrimination, and belongingness in an Ontario university environment* (Sen et al., 2025); and, 'The policy efforts to address racism and discrimination in higher education institutions: The case of Canada' (Hussain, 2023), indicate that Canadian universities lack adequate mechanisms to address racism and harassment, with neoliberal principles reinforcing racialised exclusions. The research suggests a reluctance in universities to discuss racism and the underrepresentation of racialised minorities in leadership roles. This silence extends to the lack of equity research, data collection, and specific initiatives to support racialised and Indigenous scholars, despite equity statements in job ads and university mandates (Henry et al., 2017).

Along these lines, universities continue to produce and regulate race knowledge amidst the shift from post-war liberalism to neoliberal governmentality, which has fundamentally altered the understanding and practice of equity and diversity (Henry et al., 2017). Neoliberal policies emphasise individualism and accountability, often masking structural racism and sexism. This shift has impacted the diversity of university faculty and the effectiveness of equity initiatives (Henry et al., 2017). The authors argue that neoliberalism protects the status quo by regulating who populates the academy and what work they do, resisting change and normalising Whiteness. Despite equity policies, racialised and Indigenous scholars remain marginalised (Henry et al., 2017).

The book concludes that achieving true equity requires moving away from neoliberal structures that prioritise recognising diversity and group differences. This involves collecting data to monitor progress, setting benchmarks, and implementing transparent policies. It also means challenging established norms in hiring, evaluation, and promotion to create a more inclusive academic environment (Henry et al., 2017). Together, these two works underscore the need for a fundamental rethinking of diversity and equity to address deep-seated systemic issues and achieve genuine inclusion.

Contemporary Conversations: Anti-DEI Discourse as a Continuation of Racial Oppression

January 2025 ushered in a (re)new(ed), and violent wave of anti-DEI rhetoric. This all being said, prior to the election of the new United States' president, there was a strong anti-DEI (or anti-woke) movement across the West, particularly in North America. As the following chapters in this book will explore, this positioning was not the work of one person in one moment of time, but centuries of attempts to control – and curtail – the freedoms of Black, Indigenous, and marginalised people. The power-*less*, have resisted on-going attempts of control and oppression. Unfortunately, this current battle is nothing new. What we are seeing today is how the oppressor has co-opted the language of the oppressed (e.g. the term 'woke') and uses rhetoric to undermine systemic change. The view that critical race theory (CRT) is 'racist' is a prime example.

Legislators have positioned the credibility of CRT in the US education system as a function of 'reverse racism' that is aimed at blaming White people for the 'failures' of non-Whites. However, lawmakers failed to acknowledge that CRT examines the historical and structural racism that is embedded in society, which 'privileges' Whites and those who ascribe to the tenets of Whiteness, and punishes those who do not. A similar process is happening in Canada. One of Canada's core challenges is its unwillingness to acknowledge its settler colonial past, which excluded large portions of the population as unqualified. DEI became a politicised term after 25 May 2020, when the empowerment of non-dominant groups was seen as a threat to the status quo. DEI, like multiculturalism before it, was never meant for the social mobility of non-Old Stock founding races but for others to fit within dominant structures, as Fanon (1986) argues in his *Black Skins, White Masks.* As Saini (2019) writes, 'A common theme among today's race realists is their belief that, because racial differences exist, diversity and equal opportunity programs – designed to make society fairer – are doomed to fail' (p. 85).

We must also be aware of the change and continuity of subjugation and oppression under the auspices of what I have called 'racial appeasement.' It is a space where anti-Black racism has shape-shifted through generations of practices, procedures, policies, and laws, first under the 'backdrop of slavery and colonialism, then it was immigration and segregation, and now it is the right-wing agenda of this age' (Saini, 2019, p. 84). Saini (2019) continued, stating:

> Nativism remains an issue, but there is also a backlash against greater efforts to promote racial equality in multicultural societies. And just like before, the message of those with racist intentions is tailored gently, carefully sculpted to appeal to populist fears while at the same time sounding logical and reasonable. (p. 84)

Saini (2019) points out that nativism, or the preference for 'native-born' individuals over newcomers, particularly those of darker phenotypes, continues to be a significant issue. Additionally, there is resistance against efforts to promote racial equality in multicultural societies. She emphasises that those with racist intentions craft their messages to appeal to populist fears, making them appear logical and reasonable to the public (Saini, 2019). This careful tailoring of racist rhetoric ensures its persistence and acceptance in society, despite the changing contexts. This underscores the importance of recognising and addressing the continuity of racial oppression, even as its manifestations evolve over time and through different acronyms.

Conclusion: DEI at a Crossroads

As we stand in June 2025 at the time of this writing, it is clear that DEI is at a crossroads. What began as a framework for justice and transformation has, in many cases, been diluted into a set of performative gestures – appeasement DEI that soothes White discomfort without disrupting power. Across Canada, the United States, and the United Kingdom, the language of diversity, equity, and inclusion has been co-opted, sanitised, and weaponised to maintain the very systems it was meant to challenge. Yet, history reminds us that DEI is not new. From the *Quebec Act* of 1774 to the *Civil Rights Act* of 1964, from the *Commonwealth Immigrants Act* of 1962 to *Canada's Multiculturalism Act* of 1988, the struggle for inclusion has always been entangled with the politics of race, power, and nation-building.

To move forward, we must reject the illusion that DEI is a benevolent gift from institutions. It is, and always has been, a demand – a demand for recognition, for justice, and for the reimagining of systems that have long excluded. This requires more than training sessions and symbolic hires. It demands a reckoning with colonial legacies, a dismantling of neoliberal ideologies, and a commitment to centring those who have been historically marginalised. DEI must not be about fitting into existing structures, but about transforming them. Only then can we begin to imagine a future where inclusion is not a policy, but a practice rooted in accountability, equity, and the full humanity of all.

References

Anti-Black Racism Task Force. (2021). *Report of the University of Toronto Anti-Black Racism Task Force*. https://people.utoronto.ca/wp-content/uploads/2021/04/Anti-Black-Racism-Task-Force-Report_Web.pdf

Baines, D., & Sharma, N. (2002). Migrant workers as non-citizens: The case against citizenship as a social policy concept. *Studies in Political Economy*, *69*(1), 75–107. https://doi.org/10.1080/19187033.2002.11675181

Baker, J., Lynch, K., Cantillon, S., & Walsh, J. (2004). *Equality: From theory to action* (1st ed.). Palgrave Macmillan.

Barbados Government. (1965). *Barbados: Report for the years 1962 and 1963*. Colonial Office – Barbados. https://babel.hathitrust.org/cgi/pt?id=txu.059172014250589&seq=5

Berry, J. W. (2013). Research on multiculturalism in Canada. *International Journal of Intercultural Relations*, *37*(6), 663–675. https://doi.org/10.1016/j.ijintrel.2013.09.005

Canadian Multiculturalism Act (CMA), RSC 1988, c. 24 (4th Supp.). https://laws-lois.justice.gc.ca/eng/acts/C-18.7/page-1.html

Crenshaw, K. (1989). Demarginalizing the intersection of race and sex: A Black feminist critique of antidiscrimination doctrine, feminist theory and antiracist politics. *University of Chicago Legal Forum*, *1989*(1), 139–167.

Devine, P., Kelly, G., & McAuley, M. (2022). Equality and devolution in the United Kingdom: A story in three acts and a sequel. *Social Policy and Society*, *21*(4), 612–626. https://doi.org/10.1017/S1474746421000191

Dodgson, E. (1984). *Motherland: West Indian women to Britain in the 1950s*. Heinemann Educational Books.

Fanon, F. (1986). *Black skin, white masks* C. L. Markmann, Trans. Pluto Press. (Originally published in 1952).

Freeman, G. P. (1987). Caribbean migration to Britain and France: From assimilation to selection. In B. B. Levine (Ed.), *The Caribbean exodus* (pp. 185–203). Praeger.

Government of Canada. (1969). *Statement of the Government of Canada on Indian policy*. https://publications.gc.ca/site/eng/9.700112/publication.html

Government of Canada. (1982). Section 15 – Equality rights. In *The Canadian charter of rights and freedoms*. https://www.justice.gc.ca/eng/csj-sjc/rfc-dlc/ccrf-ccdl/check/art15.html

Government of Canada. (2025, April 16). *The Canadian charter of rights and freedoms*. https://www.justice.gc.ca/eng/csj-sjc/rfc-dlc/ccrf-ccdl/index.html

Henry, F., Dua, E., James, C. E., Kobayashi, A., Li, P., Ramos, H., & Smith, M. S. (2017). *The equity myth: Racialization and Indigeneity at Canadian universities*. UBC Press.

Human Rights Code, RSO 1990, c. H.19.

Hussain, M. M. (2023). The policy efforts to address racism and discrimination in higher education institutions: The case of Canada. *Center for Educational Policy Studies Journal*, *13*(2), 9–29. https://doi.org/10.26529/cepsj.965

Iyer, A. (2022). Understanding advantaged groups' opposition to diversity, equity, and inclusion (DEI) policies: The role of perceived threat. *Social and Personality Psychology Compass*, *16*(5). Article e12666. https://doi.org/10.1111/spc3.12666

Lewis, G. K. (1990). Foreword. In R. Palmer (Ed.), *In search of a better life: Perspectives on migration from the Caribbean* (pp. xiii–xix). Bloomsbury Publishing.

Library and Archives Canada. (2024, June 22). *1774: Passage of the Quebec Act*. Office of the Commissioner of Official Languages. https://www.clo-ocol.gc.ca/en/passage-quebec-act

Mitchell, K. (2018). Identifying white mediocrity and know-your-place aggression: A form of self-care. *African American Review*, *51*(4), 253–262.

Mullings, D. V., Morgan, A., & Quelleng, H. K. (2016). Canada the great white north where anti-black racism thrives: Kicking down the doors and exposing the realities. *Phylon*, *53*(1), 20–41.

Peach, C. (1968). *West Indian migration to Britain: A social geography*. Oxford University Press.

Pryce, K. (1977). *The Black experience in Britain: A study of the life-styles of West Indians in Bristol*. University of the West Indies.

Revilla, A. T. (2021). Attempted spirit murder: Who are your spirit protectors and your spirit restorers? *The Journal of Educational Foundations*, *34*(1), 31–46.

Saini, A. (2019). *Superior: The return of race science*. Beacon Press.

Sen, R., Xue, L., Gowrikanthan, T., Masri, S., & Denis, J. (2025). *Understanding student perspectives: Racism, discrimination, and belongingness in an Ontario university environment*. McMaster University. https://msumcmaster.ca/app/uploads/2025/01/Understanding-Student-Perspectives.pdf

Simard-Côté, A. L. (2024, November 6). Conquest, compromise, and Carleton: The Quebec Act of 1774 (Season 3, Episode 1) [Audio podcast episode]. In *Voyages dans l'histoire canadienne*. The Walrus. https://thewalrus.ca/vdhc-s3e1-eng-transcript/

Taylor, C. S. (2013). *Flying fish in the great white north: The "culture" of Black Barbadian migration to 1967*. (Doctoral dissertation, University of Western Ontario). Western Electronic Thesis and Dissertation Repository. https://ir.lib.uwo.ca/etd/1525

Tessema, M. T., Hulback, T., Jones, J., Santos-Leslie, R., Ninham, K., Sterbin, A., & Swanson, N. (2023). Diversity, equity, and inclusion: History, climate, benefits, challenges, and creative strategies. *Journal of Human Resource and Sustainability Studies*, *11*(4), 780–794. https://doi.org/10.4236/jhrss.2023.114044

Thompson, D. (2025, February 8). The name can change, but the work must not: Why Canada still needs DEI. *The Globe and Mail*. https://www.theglobeandmail.com/opinion/article-the-name-can-change-but-the-work-must-not-why-canada-still-needs-dei/

Truth and Reconciliation Commission of Canada (TRC). (2015). Canada's residential schools: The history, Part 2, 1939-2000. In *The final report of the Truth and Reconciliation Commission of Canada* (Vol. 1). McGill-Queen's University Press. https://nctr.ca/wp-content/uploads/2021/01/Volume_1_History_Part_2_English_Web.pdf

UK Parliament. (n.d.). *Quebec Act 1774*. https://www.parliament.uk/about/living-heritage/evolutionofparliament/legislativescrutiny/parliament-and-empire/collections1/parliament-and-canada/quebec-act-1774/

University of Ottawa. (n.d.). *Quebec Act 1774*. Official Languages and Bilingualism Institute (OLBI). https://www.uottawa.ca/about-us/official-languages-bilingualism-institute/clmc/linguistic-history/historic-documents/quebec-act-1774

Walcott, R. (2019). The end of diversity. *Public Culture*, *31*(2), 393–408. https://doi.org/10.1215/08992363-7286885

Walcott, R. (2021). *On property: Policing, prisons, and the call for abolition*. Biblioasis.

Wang, M. L., Gomes, A., Rosa, M., Copeland, P., & Santana, V. J. (2024). A systematic review of diversity, equity, and inclusion and antiracism training studies: Findings and future directions. *Translational Behavioral Medicine*, *14*(3), 156–171. https://doi.org/10.1093/tbm/ibad061

Wolbring, G., & Nguyen, A. (2023). Equity/equality, diversity and inclusion, and other EDI phrases and EDI policy frameworks: A scoping review. *Trends in Higher Education*, *2*(1), 168–237. https://doi.org/10.3390/higheredu2010011

Appendix A: DEI Highlights From Canada, the US, and the UK

Canada: Key DEI Highlights

- *Foundational Framework:* DEI in Canada is rooted in the *Quebec Act (1774)*, which recognised religious and linguistic diversity, and later in the *Multiculturalism Policy (1971)* and *Canadian Multiculturalism Act (1988)*.
- *Legal Backbone:* The *Canadian Charter of Rights and Freedoms (1982)* enshrines equality and supports affirmative action (Section 15).
- *Multiculturalism vs. Inclusion:* Canadian DEI is often performative, used to appease rather than transform. It has historically been used to assimilate Indigenous peoples and maintain colonial structures.
- *Critiques:*
  - DEI is often used to maintain the status quo and suppress Indigenous sovereignty.
  - Rinaldo Walcott and *The Equity Myth* critique DEI as a neoliberal tool that avoids addressing systemic racism.

  - Universities lack effective mechanisms to support racialised and Indigenous scholars.
- *Contemporary Challenges:* DEI is politicised, with backlash against perceived unfairness and merit-based critiques. Anti-DEI rhetoric often masks deeper racial anxieties.

United States: Key DEI Highlights

- *Historical Milestones:*
  - *1920*: Establishment of the Women's Bureau.
  - *1941 & 1948*: Executive Orders 8802 and 9981 desegregated the military and defence industries.
  - *1960s–1970s*: *Civil Rights Act* (1964), *Equal Pay Act* (1963), and other anti-discrimination laws.
- *Corporate DEI:*
  - *1970s–2000s*: Companies began hiring for diversity and forming ERGs.
  - *2010s*: Millennials pushed for inclusive leadership.
- *Post-2020 Surge:*
  - Following George Floyd's murder, there was a wave of corporate pledges, activism, and DEI training.
- *Recent Backlash:*
  - In 2025, DEI programs faced cuts under the Trump administration, sparking national debate.
- *Critique:* DEI is often reactive and symbolic, lacking structural transformation.

United Kingdom: Key DEI Highlights

- *Evolution of DEI:*
  - Shift from 'equal opportunities' to 'diversity management' and 'inclusion management'.
  - Driven by neoliberalism and individualism, often ignoring structural inequalities.
- *Key Legislation:*
  - *Disability Discrimination Act (1995)*
  - *Race Relations Amendment Act (2000)*
  - *Equality Act (2010)*
- *Historical Context:*
  - *Commonwealth Immigrants Act (1962)* restricted non-White immigration.
  - The *Windrush Generation* faced systemic racism and exclusion.

- *Critiques:*
  - DEI is shaped by 'collective amnesia' and White supremacy.
  - Anti-Black racism and class-based exclusion are central but under-discussed.
  - DEI efforts often fail to address the root causes of inequality.
- *Contemporary Issues:*
  - Universities and institutions lack accountability and transparency in equity efforts.
  - Intersectionality is often misunderstood or ignored.

Chapter 3

A History of Blackness and DEI

What Does It Mean to Be 'Black'? DEI's Preservation of Power and Anti-Black Racism

Where slaves are free, and men oppress no more.
Fool that I was, inur'd so long to pain.
To trust to hope, or dream of joy again.
***
Now dragg'd once more beyond the western main,
To groan beneath some dastard planter's chain;
Where my poor countrymen in bondage wait
The long enfranchisement of ling'ring fate:
Hard ling'ring fate! While, ere the dawn of day,
Rous'd by the lash they go their cheerless way;
And as their souls with shame and anguish burn,
Salute with groans unwelcome morn's return,
And, chiding ev'ry hour the slow-pac'd sun,
Pursue their toils till all his race is run.
No eye to mark their suffrings with a tear;
No friend to comfort, and no hope to cheer:

Unmasking DEI, 37–50

doi:10.1108/978-1-83708-356-520261003

> Then, like the dull unpity'd brutes, repair
>
> To stalls as wretched, and as coarse a fare;
>
> Thank heaven one day of mis'ry was o'er,
>
> Then sink to sleep, and wish to wake no more.
>
> Olaudah Equiano, "The Dying Negro," 1773. (Equiano, 1790, p. 122)

We need to ponder the words of Olaudah Equiano and what it meant to be defined and created as 'Black' some 300 years ago. Equiano (1790) wrote:

> At the sight of this land [Montserrat, February 13th, 1763] of bondage, a fresh horror ran through all my frame, and chilled me to the heart. My former slavery now rose in dreadful review to my mind, and displayed nothing but misery, stripes, and chains; and, in the first paroxysm of my grief, I called upon God's thunder, and his avenging power, to direct the stroke of death to me, rather than permit me to become a slave, and be sold from lord to lord. (p. 123)

Yes, he was an enslaved person, but he was enslaved because he was labelled as Black. But what did that mean, and where did it come from, 500 years before the emergence of DEI?

Chapter 2 argued that 'DEI' as popularly practiced is frequently appeasement: representation without redistribution, inclusion as assimilation, and 'equity' stripped of power analysis. It urged us to treat diversity, equity, and inclusion as structural rather than sentimental commitments or performative actions. Building on that critique, this chapter turns to history: how Blackness was made, policed, and mobilised across empires, and how those formations seeded today's lasting DEI logics. In other words, before we can diagnose why DEI so often pacifies rather than transforms, we must reckon with the genealogy of Blackness and the political economy that made it thinkable (and profitable).

We begin with the racialising work of religious interpretation (e.g., the misread 'Curse of Ham'), followed by the later 'race-science' turn that claimed to naturalise hierarchy, and the juridical regimes that formed upon these bases. These currents predate corporate diversity by centuries, yet they established the template, an order that defines who counts as fully human, who can belong, who must assimilate, and who can be exploited. In this chapter, I trace the manifestations of this template throughout the Black Atlantic, illustrating the ways that the insidious nature of White supremacy solidified its roots in DEI 'practice'.

Making 'Blackness'? From Scriptural Misreadings to Race Science

Since 25 May 2020, we have thrown around the term 'Black,' 'anti-Black racism,' and its ultimate whitewashing to 'DEI,' but have we taken a collective mainstream 'pause' to truly understand where the roots of Blackness and Black people have come from? Historians have debated the role of the 'Curse of Ham' in justifying enslavement and racialising Black people in the New World. So, what was this infamous 'Curse of Ham'? You would need to refer to Genesis 9: 18–27 in the Bible (*King James Version*, 1611/2025), including the following excerpts:

> And the sons of Noah, that went forth from the ark, were Shem, and Ham, and Japheth; and Ham is the father of Canaan (Genesis 9:18).
>
> And he [Noah] drank of the wine, and was drunken; and he was uncovered within his tent. And Ham, the father of Canaan, saw the nakedness of his father, and told his two brethren without (Genesis 9:21).
>
> And Noah awoke from his wine, and knew what his youngest son had done unto him. And he said: Cursed be Canaan; a servant of servants shall he be unto his brethren. And he said: Blessed be the LORD, the God of Shem; and let Canaan be their servant (Genesis 9:24–27).

The 'sons' of Ham were said (misinterpreted) to be Black Africans. This passage from the Book of Genesis describes an incident involving Noah and his sons after the flood. Noah's sons, Shem, Ham, and Japheth are mentioned, with a particular focus on Ham, the father of Canaan. The narrative recounts how Noah became drunk and lay uncovered in his tent. Ham saw his father's nakedness and informed his brothers, Shem and Japheth, who then covered Noah without looking at him.

When Noah awoke and realised what had happened, he cursed Canaan, Ham's son, declaring that Canaan would be a 'servant of servants' to his brothers. Noah also blessed Shem and indicated that Canaan would serve Shem's descendants. This passage has been historically significant and controversial, particularly in its interpretation and use to justify various social and racial hierarchies. The Curse of Ham has been misinterpreted over centuries to rationalise the enslavement and subjugation of Black people, despite the text itself not explicitly mentioning race or skin colour. The curse is directed at Canaan, not Ham, and the reasons for the curse are rooted in the cultural and familial context of the time. Overall, the passage serves as a reminder of how religious texts can be interpreted in various ways, often influenced by the socio-political context of the interpreters. It underscores the importance of critical analysis and awareness of historical misinterpretations that have had lasting impacts on societies.

While some scholars, like Stanley Harrold and Michael Banton, have downplayed its significance, others, including David Brion Davis, David Goldenberg, Benjamin Brand, Jonathan Schorsch, and Anton L. Allahar, have highlighted its misinterpretations as a basis for Black oppression. Davis (2006) argued that the Biblical text itself does not directly link to race or colour, but the enslavement of Africans transformed its meaning, making it central to anti-Black racism and enslavement. Goldenberg (2003) supported this view, noting that biblical commentators often ignored the text's actual wording. Braude (2003) suggested that the Curse of Ham might be linked to Asia, while Schorsch (2004) pointed out that Jewish discourse used it to explain Blackness and justify enslavement.

The negative ideology of Blackness predates the Transatlantic Slave Trade, with mediaeval art and thought linking Blackness to inferiority (Friedman, 1998). This historical context facilitated the creation of stereotypes associating darker skin with negative traits (Davis, 2006). Allahar and Côté (1998) argued that this process led to Blackness signifying inferiority, supported by the Curse of Ham and Christian ideology. Several scholars, including Eric Williams (1994), Jack Gratus (1973), Edmund Morgan (2003), and Peter Kolchin (2003), have implicated religion and Christian doctrine in justifying Black African enslavement. Gratus (1973) noted that Biblical interpretations, such as those by Reverend Raymund Harris, supported enslavement, while abolitionists like William Wilberforce believed in converting Black heathens to Christianity. Kolchin (2003) discussed religious arguments that justified chattel enslavement, including the Curse of Ham and the idea that enslavement exposed heathens to Christianity's blessings.

How 'Difference' Shifts From Theology to Biology to Policy

Angela Saini (2019), in her book *Superior: The Return of Race Science,* recounts her experiences throughout its chapters: walking through a museum, viewing a natural wonder, riding a rollercoaster ride, visiting a library, a trip to another country, and many more. These experiences, however, are not just a narrative retelling of her personal history; rather, they are different spaces where race science is present in both historical legacy and present practice. Race science, according to Saini (2019), refers to the ways that science, founded on White supremacy, defined race through undeniable and immovable differences in groups of people that set them apart. For example, Johann Friedrich Blumenbach (1795), a German doctor, categorised humanity into five 'varieties' in his book *On the Natural Variety of Mankind.* These categories included Caucasians, Mongolians, Ethiopians, Americans, and Malays. Blumenbach's (1795) definition of Caucasians was broad, encompassing people from Europe, India, and North Africa. Saini (2019) also addresses Canadian race science, citing John Philippe Rushton, a psychology professor at Western University, who controversially linked brain and genital size to intelligence and race.

Race science, which has long been debunked but nevertheless remains, created a power hierarchy that cuts across time and space, placing White Europeans at the top, viewing themselves as the natural successors of ancient civilisations (Saini, 2019). Saini highlighted Martin Porr. Porr, a German archaeologist at the University of Western Australia, critiqued the Enlightenment for reinforcing the idea of human unity while being shaped by European colonial perspectives. In their work, the author also wrote about Jonathan Marks. Marks, an anthropology professor at the University of North Carolina, Charlotte, argues that race science emerged from colonial ideologies aimed at classifying and controlling people. Saini (2019) explored Marks' argument that race science continues to persist because it serves political purposes, with powerful right-wing forces funding research to justify inequalities. By 1949, the focus of race science shifted towards social construction, with academics acknowledging that race was not a reliable way to understand human variation. UNESCO's (1950) statement on race emphasised that all humans belong to the same species, *Homo sapiens*.

Saini (2019) concludes that politics is inherently tied to the science of race, reflecting on her own experiences growing up in southeast London, where non-White individuals were often categorised as Black, marking them for differential treatment and surveillance. Along similar lines, Hilary Beckles (2013), in his book *Britain's Black Debt: Reparations for Caribbean Slavery and Native Genocide*, discusses the dehumanisation of Africans under British colonial rule. He explains that the British legally classified Africans as 'nonhuman', considering them a subspecies at best. This classification justified the creation of special laws for their governance and economic exploitation, treating them as 'beasts of burden' and property (Beckles, 2013, p. 56). Ta-Nehisi Coates (2024) continued, noting that 'the first duty of racism, sexism, homophobia, and so forth is the framing of who is human and who is not' (p. 148). Joanne Pope Melish (2000) argued that enslavement was 'a relationship structured by kinship (either inclusively or, more persuasively, exclusively) in which the rights of one class of human beings to reproductive and other social relationships, personhood, and labour have assigned to another person or persons' (p. 25). These humans are dehumanised and 'rendered kinless, depersonalised, and transformed into *things*, with the ratification of the law. This legal transformation ensures access to their labour in perpetuity and also the permanence of their strangerhood' (Melish, 2000, p. 25, emphasis in original). Black identity was, and is, constructive in particularly subjugated ways that renders an entire population's identity as power-*less* objects to be owned by the power-*full*. This essentialisation of Blackness and Black identity puts Black people at an unfair disadvantage. One where they are either human or they are not.

The Black Atlantic as Laboratories of Racial Capitalism: 'Inclusion' as **Permission,** *not* **Power**

Shifting the narrative, Paul Gilroy's (1995) concepts of the ship and the Black Atlantic, support a global and transnational view of Black identity. Gilroy (1995) argues that creolisation, the ship, and the Atlantic Ocean played key roles in shaping Black identity in the Western world. These historical and modern movements created Black identities that did not fit neatly into traditional ideas of modernity and nationality. Instead, a sense of national and diasporic belonging emerged without strict political boundaries. Gilroy's (1995) ideas encourage us to rethink and reimagine Black identity formation, considering the transnational connections of racial attitudes throughout the British Empire. This is supported by Barbadian (Bajan) scholar Jo-Anne Tull (2017), as she argues that:

> much of the Caribbean's future is contingent on what we as Caribbean people perceive of ourselves (identity), what we believe we have and can give (indigenous resources), and therefore how we might consistently use these elements to contribute to the region's future growth (sustainability). (p. 294)

I believe that this historical context is crucial to understanding the long-standing perception of Black people in Western societies and our relationship with DEI. As Tull (2017) writes, self-identification shapes Caribbean prosperity. I believe that without (un)learning our true Black *Self*, one that sits in the truth of enslavement and colonisation, but is not bound by its histories, we can – and will – move forward as a people. However, we must understand how our present-day realities have been shaped by these oppressive and violent histories. For nearly 200 years after the end of legal enslavement in British colonies in 1834, Black people were not recognised as fully human. This historical dehumanisation has influenced contemporary attitudes and resistance to DEI programs. White individuals may resist these programs because they still subconsciously view Black people as less than human, while Black individuals may embrace them to assert their humanity within systems that have historically denied it, despite these programs' shortcomings. This creates a paradox wherein efforts to promote equality are met with resistance rooted in a long history of dehumanisation. But what does this all mean for the 20th century? For the 21st century? What does this idea of Blackness look and feel like for prominent and lesser-known Black people across the Black Atlantic?

As one of Canada's pre-eminent Black leaders who, however, was not widely known outside of the province of Nova Scotia, Burnley 'Rocky' Jones' autobiography was a lesson in experiencing and understanding the made-in-Canada form of anti-Black racism (Jones & Walker, 2016). This, I believe, is bedrock for how we can understand and contextualise the passive aggressive ethos of DEI in Canada. The 'I can tolerate you being here, as long as you keep your mouth shut and stay in your place' type of diversity, equity, and inclusion. In the 1950s, after being told that he couldn't play a game of pool at a hall, he recalled, 'I was just 13 and the guy has dehumanised me, he just cut the balls right off of me, standing there in front of my friends' (Jones & Walker, 2016, p. 27). He pointedly states something that is often in the debates of DEI, those both for and against it: the element of power. Institutionalised power. DEI initiatives put in place without addressing, challenging, and transforming the institutional power dynamics of anti-Black racism are useless. Power, embedded in laws and violence, facilitated the Transatlantic Slave Trade, the enslavement of Black people, and the ways these continue to resonate today. Jones, as a kid, may not have been able to articulate this feeling as child with big fancy academic words, but he knew that, 'in order to be racist you have to have power of the institution to back your play, but when they came into our programme there was no power in the institution for that kind of thing' (Jones & Walker, 2016, p. 179). He knew that:

> was someone who has power over me, he's got physical power, he's got the power of the state because he owns the place. He's got all this power, and he's exercising this power over me. I was helpless... I'll never forget that until the day I die. (Jones & Walker, 2016, p. 28)

Indeed, Coates (2024), a Black American, writing in the backlash of the sweeping 'anti-woke' movement in the Americas, made us all remember, 'Race is a species of power and nothing else' (p. 126).

Along these lines, Jones sums up the relationship of DEI and anti-Black racism in Canada, and I would say the view of DEI across the US, Canada, and the UK, perfectly with this statement:

> This is the strange nature of Canadian racism. There are these little pockets of openings that are making people feel better who are exercising power, exercising power, exercising discrimination. They say, 'Okay we will let you have this much, and these others will have nothing. But as long as we can say we let so and so have this much, we are not bad people and don't you accuse us of this or that'. (Jones & Walker, 2016, p. 28)

Jones articulates that Canadian racism operates in a way that allows those in power to feel good about themselves while still exercising discrimination. They create small allowances for some, which they use to deflect accusations of racism, maintaining a system that is 'totally a 100% racist but in a way that doesn't look racist' (Jones & Walker, 2016, p. 29). Think about that statement. Think about how it is possible that Canada, the supposed 'least' racist country of the three, the only one that has officially enshrined the precursor to DEI – multiculturalism – in law, along with every Canadian's charter rights, could be 100% racist without looking the part? I would add that it is not just racism, but particularly anti-Black racism. It is our collective consciousness lulled to sleep, covered by the cloak of progress, as we are stabbed with the dagger of anti-Blackism. Jones' reflections are crucial for understanding the limitations of DEI initiatives that do not address the underlying power structures. His experiences illustrate how institutional power perpetuates racism, making superficial DEI efforts insufficient. This analysis is relevant not only in Canada but also in the US and the UK, where similar dynamics exist. Jones' insights, and the experiences long shared by Black, Indigenous, and racialised people and scholars, call for a deeper examination of how power is distributed and exercised within institutions and the need for genuine transformation to achieve true equity and inclusion. So how did we get here? From the Curse of Ham, to Enslavement, to anti-Black racism in pool halls, to anti-woke and DEI? We need to go back to the myth of White supremacy and the centuries-old roots of DEI.

The Long Historical Road to DEI

The 'Misinterpretation' of White Supremacy

In early 2020, I was interviewed by a local newspaper in Canada. The interviewer asked about my thoughts and feelings around White supremacy. I told him that:

> White supremacy is not you as an individual – the tiki torches, burning crosses. There's no more lynching.
>
> But White supremacy as a system is alive and well. Our education system is founded on it, our justice system. Federal inmates are 30% Indigenous. Somebody explain that one to me. There's a water crisis in Indigenous communities. Black folks are shot by the cops. It's not one individual bad apple when it keeps happening and happening. (Rubinoff, 2020, para. 32–33)

What I mean by this is clear in the words of scholar Frances Lee Ansley (1989), who wrote:

> By "White supremacy" I do not mean to allude only to the self-conscious racism of White supremacist hate groups. I refer instead to a political, economic and cultural system in which Whites overwhelmingly control power and material resources, conscious and unconscious ideas of White superiority and entitlement are widespread, and relations of White dominance and non-White subordination are daily re-enacted across a broad array of institutions and social settings. (p. 1024)

Ansley (1989) continued, 'If privilege and racism are the symptoms, White supremacy is the disease' (p. 1024).

In *Mediocre: The Dangerous Legacy of White Male America*, Ijeoma Oluo (2020) wrote that, 'White supremacy is, and has always been, a pyramid scheme' (p. 131); a scheme based on the idea that all White people, including those in Canada, the United States and across British colonies in the Americas, owned enslaved peoples. In fact, in the United States, only 25% of Southern White households owned enslaved peoples and 7% owned the majority of enslaved people (Oluo, 2020). To rub salt in the wound, the term 'White trash' may have come from Black enslaved people to describe 'poor Whites doing the dirty work of wealthy slave owners' (Oluo, 2020, p. 132). In essence, if White people truly understood that there are class-based and socio-economic levels to their ascription as power-*full*, they would begin to understand that their true nemesis is not a Black DEI-hire or a newcomer coming to 'steal' their jobs. The power-*full* class needs to create race-fuelled discord among the 'mixed-race' proletariat in order for them to maintain their hegemonic control in society. These insights highlight the pervasive and systemic nature of White supremacy, emphasising the need for a deeper understanding and active dismantling of these entrenched structures. What we need now is a clear timeline of where this 'myth of White supremacy' begins. The story begins with a White settler in the 13 colonies in the 17th century.

From Emancipation to Multiculturalism: Antislavery, Liberal Reform, and the Emergence of Administrative 'Equality' Regimes that Sidestep Redistribution

In *American Slavery, American Freedom*, Edmund S. Morgan (2003) discusses the response to Indigenous threats in Virginia on 7 March 1676. The assembly decided to build forts and establish a standing army, which seemed more like an opportunity for profiteering than a genuine defence measure (Morgan, 2003). Nathaniel Bacon, a young newcomer with interests in the fur trade, set up a plantation and felt disdain for wealthy Virginians who had risen from humble beginnings or public funds (Morgan, 2003). Frustrated by the lack of support from the Virginia assembly, Bacon declared that the country must defend itself against all Indigenous people, whom he considered enemies (Morgan, 2003).

Bacon's rebellion involved waging war against both friendly and hostile Indigenous communities, eventually turning against the ruling elite. During the insurrection, he offered freedom to the servants and Black enslaved people of loyalists (Morgan, 2003). At the rebellion's end, 80 enslaved people and 20 English servants refused to surrender (Morgan, 2003). Morgan notes that if disappointed White freemen allied with desperate enslaved Black people, the consequences could be dire and essentially destabilise the class hierarchy (Morgan, 2003). The solution, though unspoken, was anti-Black racism, which separated free Whites from enslaved Blacks through racial contempt (Morgan, 2003). Bacon himself demonstrated the social utility of racism, directing his prejudice primarily against Indigenous peoples rather than Blacks (Morgan, 2003). You can see how Bacon, and not for benevolent reasons, was the first to promote a foundational framework of diversity, equity, and inclusion. Mind you, it was to oppress Indigenous Peoples and overthrow the ruling elite, but he understood that the issue at hand was not Black and White, but power against a ruling elite.

To complement Morgan's work, Peter Kolchin (2003), in *American Slavery, 1619–1877*, explains that the initial demand for labour, which eventually led to enslavement, was not based on race. The settler colonists came from a hierarchical society that did not clearly distinguish between free and unfree statuses as the modern world does (Kolchin, 2003). Over time, differences emerged as Africans were perceived as 'Black', associated with being 'dirty' and 'immoral', while Europeans were seen as 'White' and pure. Those in the African Continent were also labelled as 'savage' or 'uncivilised' and 'heathens' for not being Christian. This perception persisted even after laws allowed the enslavement of Black Christians (Kolchin, 2003).

Throughout much of the 17th century, Black people were treated only slightly differently from other lower-class individuals (Kolchin, 2003). The brutal repression of unruly elements in Britain and the colonisation of Ireland preceded the English assault on Indigenous Peoples in the Americas and the enslavement of Black Africans, showing that race alone does not explain these policies (Kolchin, 2003). The English gentry viewed their lower classes and the Irish similarly, considering them ignorant and brutish, requiring physical repression (Kolchin, 2003).

Following Bacon's Rebellion in 1676, planters became increasingly concerned about controlling unruly labourers. Both enslaved people and servants who ran away faced severe punishments, including whippings, mutilations, and extended servitude for servants. Eighteenth-century colonial newspapers were filled with advertisements for runaway fugitives, both White and Black (Kolchin, 2003). Morgan (2003) also explores class consciousness, noting that stereotypes of the poor in England mirrored descriptions of Blacks in 'slavocracies', suggesting dehumanisation for both groups (p. 325). Legislation could substitute class for colour, as seen in a 1697 *Act* requiring poor relief recipients to wear a marked 'P' (Morgan, 2003, p. 326).

Social prestige was linked to both Whiteness and wealth, leading to confusion over whether prejudice was due to colour or poverty (Morgan, 2003). In *Many Thousands Gone: The First Two Centuries of Slavery in North America*, Ira Berlin (1998) describes how Black and White people often enjoyed each other's company in the 17th century. They would secretly drink, gamble, and have fun together, away from the eyes of slaveholders (Berlin, 1998). Berlin notes that most 'mixed-race' children in the Chesapeake region came from relationships between enslaved Black people and White servants, not from White planters imposing on Black women (Berlin, 1998). Poor people of different races often trusted each other and worked together to challenge their superiors; they would run away together, plot minor conspiracies, and sometimes stand united against the authorities (Berlin, 1998).

What we must remember here is that Barbados, the 17th-century jewel in the eye of the English and British, was the epicentre of what we can now call 'race relations.' English and British sensibilities of Black people and Blackness, ideas that we think are firmly products of the '40 acres and a mule' anti-Blackness of the United States, were imported from the Caribbean, specifically Barbados. The first enslaved people who were shipped to Virginia in 1619 did not come directly from the African continent, but from Barbados (Morgan, 2003).

The DEI Prequel: Yesterday's Governance of Blackness to Today's Performance of Inclusion

We must engage with this knowledge of race and racism, as I argue is the case with DEI, through the eyes of understanding, not colour, but class, power dynamics, and control over labour. Moreover, I argue here that precisely because of enslavement and the dehumanising anti-Black racism that justified the system, it created the groundwork for the ideological principles of DEI. Scholar David Brion Davis (2006) stated:

> There is a profound historical irony, or some might say evidence of God's design, in the fact that the birth of Britain's slave plantation economy in the West Indies coincided in time with Britain's domestic civil war of the 1640s, in which radical religious groups challenged all forms of oppression and privilege, including private property, and established the theological foundation for the much later antislavery movements. (p. 114)

This is a prime example of how Black enslavement was used as the foundation for 'social justice' and DEI. Why? We, in the 2020s, have the mainstream understanding that DEI fights oppression and facilitates equal rights. Barbados was the first and leading source for English, and then, British plantocracies and enslavement, with its first big rise from 1640–1643, which coincided with 17th-century 'social justice' movements in England. Indeed, it is the first country in the Americas whose sole purpose for existence was to create White wealth through the brutal dehumanisation and death of Black people. Richard S. Dunn (1972) summed it up quite well, writing that Barbados was 'the richest and yet in human terms the least successful colony in English America'. Barbados 'had lost most of the reassuring social and psychological boundaries of traditional societies' (as cited in Davis, 2006, p. 115).

As the pre-eminent scholar of enslavement in the British Caribbean, Eric Eustace Williams (1994) wrote:

> Slavery in the Caribbean has been too narrowly identified with the Negro. A racial twist has thereby been given to what is basically an economic phenomenon. Slavery was not born of racism: rather, racism was the consequence of slavery. Unfree labour in the New World was brown, White, black, yellow; Catholic, Protestant and pagan. (p. 7)

He continued, stating that Black enslavement's origins can be expressed in three words: in the Caribbean, Sugar; on the mainland, Tobacco and Cotton. A change in the economic structure produced a corresponding change in the labour supply' (Williams, 1994, p. 23). The historical 'narrow' definition of enslavement is akin to the misunderstandings of *who* DEI is *for*. If present-day society understood class-based concepts of power, including who is power-*full* or who is power-*less*, as opposed to obfuscated terms of 'middle class,' they would have a better understanding that DEI – if done ethically – could overthrow power structures that oppress all colours of the rainbow.

The DEI 'project' of inclusion, or assimilation, was a founding fabric of the Americas, rooted in British sensibilities. It was the wealth, greed, and a need to maintain power by the ruling (White) elite that created real and imagined boundaries. One could argue that, and the writers of the United States Constitution would agree, that you can't have (White) social justice and 'freedoms' without oppressing (Black) others. The irony, as Davis (2006) writes, is how the learnt 'theological foundation' went on to support antislavery movements 150 years later. We cannot have conversations about the roots of DEI without engaging the histories of enslavement, anti-Black racism, and the origins of Barbados as the first slavocracy. It is only by working through these foundational structures that we can understand the DEI movement in the contemporary neoliberal state we find ourselves in, one which promotes merit, excellence, and possibility without ever addressing the root causes of anti-Black racism that preclude whole groups of people from these ostensible benefits. What a world we would live in almost 400 years later if Bacon succeeded and Black and White people united as one. Historical insights from scholars like Eric Wiliams, David Brion Davis, Edmund S. Morgan, Peter Kolchin, and Ira Berlin reveal that systemic racism and class divisions have long been entrenched in society. If Bacon's rebellion had succeeded, it might have united Black and White people against the ruling elite, potentially altering the course of history and addressing these deep-seated issues. Critical moments in history, particularly histories that we are a part of, such as 25 May 2020, have the potential to alter our societies for the better. However, as we will see, White supremacy is the weight that continues to pull us under the tides of the Atlantic. Gasping for air. Hoping for breath. Pleading for life.

Conclusion

This chapter traced how Blackness was made governable through scripture, science, and the state, and how empires translated that governability into wealth, law, and ideology. The story teaches that inclusion without power is not a mistake; it is a design feature of the racial order wherein those in positions of power learnt they could manage dissent through recognition without redistribution. That is why contemporary DEI so often feels like a polite no: it names difference while keeping decision rights intact.

Through the Caribbean plantation complex (with Barbados as a crucible), the British Atlantic forged racial categories tethered to labour extraction. The result was not only material dispossession but also a moral and epistemic order in which 'Black' was cast as deficient and dangerous, while 'inclusion' appeared as conditional tolerance under White sovereignty. This historical arc clarifies why contemporary DEI so easily slides into performative inclusion that leaves power untouched.

Moments of multiracial solidarity and anti-colonial insurgency (from Bacon's Rebellion to 20th-century movements) were repeatedly neutralised by strategies that re-secure legitimacy without restructuring power. The multicultural and equal opportunity frameworks of the late 20th century inherit these contradictions; they recode colonial management as 'inclusion' while preserving advantage. The analytical payoff is simple: today's DEI is legible as a continuity – not a rupture – in the governance of Black life.

The next chapter picks up at a familiar breaking point; when Black resistance becomes audible at scale (e.g., 2020), institutions counter with paternalistic recognition, programmatic DEI, and then a sharp anti-DEI backlash. Chapter 4 theorises this oscillation as the Negro-Apocalypse – a lens for understanding how the threat of unapologetic Blackness produces cycles of appeasement, co-optation, and punishment.

References

Allahar, A. H., & Côté, J. E. (1998). *Richer and poorer: The structure of inequality in Canada.* James Lorimer & Company.

Ansley, F. L. (1989). Stirring the ashes: Race, class and the future of civil rights scholarship. *Cornell Law Review*, *74*, 993–1077. https://scholarship.law.cornell.edu/clr/vol74/iss6/1

Beckles, H. M. (2013). *Britain's Black debt: Reparations for Caribbean slavery and Native genocide.* The University of the West Indies Press.

Berlin, I. (1998). *Many thousands gone: The first two centuries of slavery in North America.* Harvard University Press.

Blumenbach, J. H. (1795). *On the natural variety of mankind* (De generis humani varietate nativa) (3rd ed.). Vandenhoek.

Braude, B. (2003). Ham and Noah: Sexuality, servitudinism, and ethnicity. In *Proceedings of the Fifth Annual Glider Lehrman Center International Conference at Yale University.* Yale University. https://glc.yale.edu/sites/default/files/files/events/race/Braude.pdf

Coates, T. N. (2024). *The message.* BCP Literary.

Davis, D. B. (2006). *Inhuman bondage: The rise and fall of slavery in the new world.* Oxford University Press.

Dunn, R. S. (1972). *Sugar and slaves: The rise of the planter class in the English West Indies, 1624–1713.* University of North Carolina Press (for the Institute of Early American History and Culture).

Equiano, O. (1790). *The interesting narrative of the life of Olaudah Equiano, or Gustavus Vassa, the African* (3rd ed.). Self-published. https://equianosworld.org/assets/files/3rd%20Edition%20-%20The%20Interesting%20Narrative.pdf

Friedman, S. S. (1998). *Jews and the American slave trade.* Transaction Publishers.

Gilroy, P. (1995). *The Black Atlantic: Modernity and double-consciousness.* Harvard University Press.

Goldenberg, D. M. (2003). *The Curse of Ham: Race and slavery in early Judaism, Christianity, and Islam.* Princeton University Press.

Gratus, J. (1973). *The great white lie: Slavery, emancipation, and changing racial attitudes.* Monthly Review Press.

Jones, B. R., & Walker, J. W. S. G. (2016). *Burnley "Rocky" Jones revolutionary: An autobiography by Burnley "Rocky" Jones*. Fernwood Publishing.

King, J. B. (2025). *King James Bible Online*. (Originally published in 1611). https://www.kingjamesbibleonline.org/

Kolchin, P. (2003). *American slavery: 1619–1877* (10th anniv. ed.). University of North Carolina Press.

Melish, J. P. (2000). *Disowning slavery: Gradual emancipation and "race" in New England, 1780–1860*. Cornell University Press.

Morgan, E. S. (2003). *American slavery, American freedom* (Rev. ed.). WW Norton.

Oluo, I. (2020). *Mediocre: The dangerous legacy of White male America*. Seal Press.

Rubinoff, J. (2020, February 28). *At the end of the day, even when I'm on campus, I'm a Black guy, full stop!* Waterloo Region Record. https://www.therecord.com/news/waterloo-region/at-the-end-of-the-day-even-when-im-on-campus-im-a-black-guy/article_ac33a670-5cc2-5ba2-b00d-69c5c81434d9.html

Saini, A. (2019). *Superior: The return of race science*. Beacon Press.

Schorsch, J. (2004). *Jews and Blacks in the early modern world*. Cambridge University Press.

Tull, J. A. (2017). Caribbean festival arts: Exploring praxis for the future. *Caribbean Quarterly*, *63*(2–3), 291–303. https://doi.org/10.1080/00086495.2017.1352278

UNESCO. (1950). *The race question. UNESCO and its programme* (Part 3. pp. 1–11). https://unesdoc.unesco.org/ark:/48223/pf0000128291

Williams, E. E. (1994). *Capitalism & slavery*. The University of North Carolina Press.

Chapter 4

The Negro-Apocalypse

From Appeasement to Backlash: A Recurring Pattern

Chapters 2–3 showed how DEI's modern vocabulary sits atop historically established infrastructures that police Black life while preserving elite control. Chapter 4 names the latest rupture: the post-2020 Negro-Apocalypse, a period when mass recognition of anti-Black violence met a swift counter-movement to restore order, through symbolic inclusion, policy rollbacks and narrative warfare.

Why 'Apocalypse'? A Theory of the Cycle

I did not choose to term this point in time as an 'Apocalypse' lightly. Rather, I chose this term *because* it is deliberately jarring: it points to a crisis for White identity and institutional legitimacy whenever Black humanity refuses assimilation. It signals revelation; institutions and publics briefly saw what Black communities have long known: the architecture of their safety is built on Black precarity. The response was twofold: (1) rapid investments in DEI optics (e.g. committees, cluster hires, pledges) and (2) a coordinated anti-DEI turn that shuttered offices, banned curricula and reframed equity as 'reverse discrimination'. The chapter argues that both moves – care and subsequent crackdown – serve the same function; re-securing hierarchy while narrating progress.

Drawing on Baldwin and Freire, we trace the ways the discovery of oneself as an oppressor produces *paternalism* rather than solidarity, and 'inclusion' becomes a site for laundering rage. Further, we explore the ways some Black leaders adopt shadow strategies, using the DEI aperture to build durable networks that outlast the news cycle. This is not a morality tale, it is a power analysis of how institutions metabolize a veritable ending of the world as they knew it.

Unmasking DEI, 51–63

doi:10.1108/978-1-83708-356-520261004

The Black Oppressed and the Negro-Apocalypse: When Black Voice Rises, Institutions Reach for Containment

25 May 2020 reignited a fear of Black unrest among Black people in White spaces. Unrest that dates back to 1444 with the forced removal of the first African peoples from the Continent as chattel to Lagos, Portugal. The fearless violent battles against enslavement in Tacky's War in Jamaica 1760; the 1816 Bussa Rebellion in Barbados; the Jamaican 1865 Morant Bay Rebellion; the 1919 UK Race Riots; the unrests of the 1969 Sir George Williams Affair in Quebec; the 1992 Yonge Street Rebellion in Canada and Rodney King riots in the United States (US); and the countless other documented and undocumented liberation and emancipation movements.

Society needed to 'stop' the racial (re)awakening of Black Power in the 2020s; a sensibility reignited in a new generation of oppressed peoples. I have termed this period of time, the Negro-Apocalypse. I am aware that this term may be jarring to some; however, the term Negro (no conflation with the inflammatory 'n-word') is rooted in the late 19th and early 20th century denigration and classification of the colonized 'Black' subaltern. It is key to revert to this historical language to contextualize the violent resistance of Black liberation in the 21st century. As James Baldwin (1993) wrote in *The Fire Next Time*, 'the [B]lack man has functioned in the white man's world as a fixed star, as an immovable pillar: and as he moves out of his place, heaven and earth are shaken to their foundations' (p. 9). We ask in the mid-2020s why there is such a severe backlash against DEI; well, it is precisely because there is/was a fear that White people were losing a piece of their identity. It was not just the idea of them losing power, or a seat at the boardroom table, or having to sit through an unconscious bias session as they scrolled through their Truth Social app.

It was, as Baldwin wrote decades ago, their foundation – their core identity – was now being challenged with truth and facts. As Paulo Freire (1970) wrote in *Pedagogy of the Oppressed*, the visceral reactions we saw in the classrooms, boardrooms, social media and news articles were the oppressor finally discovering their true identity, as an oppressor. Freire (1970) said:

> Discovering himself to be an oppressor may cause considerable anguish, but it does not necessarily lead to solidarity with the oppressed. Rationalizing his guilt through paternalistic treatment of the oppressed, all the while holding them fast in a position of dependence, will not do. (p. 23)

There was the misbelief (fleeting hope?) of the oppressed, the Black oppressed, that the moment that 8 minutes and 46 seconds ended, the White oppressed would see their faults. They would see the truth and reconcile. They would change and be better people, be a more diverse, equitable and inclusive society that would benefit all shapes, sizes and colours. Those of us that had been in the game long before 2020 knew that this was a hope, not a reality. We knew, as soon as conversations quickly shifted from confronting and challenging anti-Black racism towards the Neville Chamberlain policy of appeasement of 21st century DEI, we were doomed. They rationalized their anti-Black guilt by invoking 'what-aboutisms': 'What about other groups that faced oppression? What about all the other –isms? What about this? What about that?' Meanwhile, corporate CEOs, university presidents and elected officials across the Atlantic held out the hand of paternalism: creating the DEI committees, pushing forward some DEI contracts, hiring a few DEI consultants to 'fix' the problem. The challenge was, and is, that some of the (well-meaning Black) oppressed:

> have internalized the image of the oppressor and adopted his guidelines, are fearful of freedom. Freedom would require them to eject this image and replace it with autonomy and responsibility. (Freire, 1970, p. 21)

Freire (1970) continues that this process is unavoidable, an 'indispensable condition for the quest for human completion' (p. 21). DEI became the pinnacle of 'freedom' and the 'human completion', but as I wrote in Chapter 3, DEI frameworks, particularly in Canada, have historically defined and controlled non-White bodies under the auspices of 'freedom' and 'liberation'. Ultimately, it created a spectacle of Fanonian neo-colonial Black skins, with White masks; a space where DEI offices, many that were headed by Black skins, had to don White masks (or, adhere to dominant White power structures) in order to push through performative 'unconscious bias' training sessions and 'inclusive hiring' programmes that did little to move the needle on Black empowerment. If these leaders ventured too far off the plantation without massa's permission, they would be whipped.

Recognition Without Redistribution in the 2020 'Wave': Pledges, Hires and Trainings That Soothed Conscience but Preserved Structure

Unfortunately, these initiatives, as we have seen with the hindsight of 20/20 vision, were actually akin to the powers that be throwing scraps to a hungry dog under the table; not even to fill our bellies, but enough to stop of us from begging until they could finish their four-course meals. A cluster hire of 10 Black professors is only a statistical rounding error for an organization of 5,000 employees that only had 5 Black tenured academics in 2019. A series of corporations signing on to a pledge to address anti-Black racism does not change the socioeconomic disparities of Black youth. Creating a DEI office headed by Black people that could not focus solely on Black oppression – less they create the perception of an Oppression Olympics by seemingly ignoring the plight of all students, staff, faculty and employees – is a core and deliberate failure of DEI. The language and positioning of DEI – or All Lives Matter frameworks – made the (Black) oppressed dependent on the time-limited goodwill and budgets of the overseer, massa and colonial agent. Right before our eyes, the ostensible benevolence of DEI reverted Black Lives Matter (BLM), the humanity of Black lives, to a position of control and dependence of what the oppressor was comfortable with, and created themselves; the Negro.

However, the Negro was no longer a Negro. In 2020, we could have been shouting: 'We are not your Negroes!' We are not the dehumanized being that thought we should *always* be. The Book of Revelation describes the Apocalypse as the complete destruction of the world (King James Bible, 1611/2025). In this case, 25 May 2020 ushered in a platform for the possibility of the complete destruction of the White world. The world was listening and seeing a fundamentally anti-Black world, a world built on lies, greed and violence; a world defined by, as Dr King Jr. stated, the 'thingification' of Blackness and Black bodies. However, what we began to see in 2020 was the awakening, the *wokeness*, of the masses; the masses opening their eyes to the lies that they had been fed for generations. They began to see the proverbial house of cards of Whiteness, full of refined sugar-laden empty calories that ultimately leads to chronic illness.

We always must remember that post-2020, DEI came in to 'white wash' the focus on confronting anti-Black racism. DEI was instituted to quiet Black voices; it came to be to silence the Black voice, and appease the Negro. The colonized Negro was the personification of White 'superiority' and Black 'servitude'. To be committed to Black focused anti-colonialism, liberation and emancipation, is 'to be in danger' as it not only challenges colonial systems, but a collective 'White' sense of Self (Baldwin, 1993, p. 9). To do anti-Black racism work, which was quickly supplanted in word (not necessarily in deed) to BIPOC and DEI, was to be in danger. Our ways of thinking, being and living, were and *are* in danger. And from what we have seen in the mid-2020s, our careers and livelihoods were and are too.

In Canada, the ways that Black people are surveilled and punished for stepping 'out of line' have long embedded roots. The early twentieth-century Canadian fear of Black men violating the sanctity of White womanhood pulls on these same threads. The historical narrative flows through to the dehumanized hypersexualization and adultification of young Black girls that led to the shackling of melanated toddlers in the new 21st century. We may not be your Negro, but colonial systems will do everything in their power to remind you who they want you to be.

I need us all to pause and think about what I just wrote for a second. As Freire (1970) wrote, 'for cultural invasion to succeed, it is essential that those invaded become convinced of their intrinsic inferiority' (p. 126). To be centred as a 'Negro', whether through name or actions, harkens back to my discussion of the demonization of Black people as a means to oppress and control in Chapter 3. 'Black' means *power-full*; 'Negro' means *power-less*. It is not to be mistaken that to be a Negro, a colonized being, you did not have any agency or autonomy, no. It means that your being, and your Self, was dictated by the dehumanization of Black bodies, made possible through the Transatlantic Slave Trade, enslavement and colonization.

The Anti-DEI Turn: Office Closures, Curricular Bans and Narrative Inversion ('Reverse Racism') as Counter-Revolution

It is critically important for us to situate this language within the conversations of DEI. The premise of the (anti-)DEI movement is that irrespective of the intersections of race, gender, class, etc., we (the citizens of a particularly 'imagined' nation-state) are ideologically and legally 'equal'. From this perspective, historical wrongs, the language we use or even legal facts should not be taken into account at present because it all happened 'a long time ago' and we need to 'get over it'. This approach understands the legal ending of enslavement in England in 1772, across Canada and British colonies in 1834, and the US (officially) in 1865, as the ending of the egregious forms of anti-Black racism. Thus, we are all now equal, and any measure of support for the centuries of oppression before and after the legal ending of legislated anti-Black racism should not be taken into account. This is one key premise of the anti-DEI movement. Therefore, when I write here about the Negro and the Negro-Apocalypse, you can begin to understand how this collective memory of a goldfish of a (White) anti-DEI society is so troublesome. Unlike goldfish, however, our society is not biologically pre-disposed to memory loss. Rather, this is intentional.

On top of that, we can begin to see how troubling 'simple' book removals, critical race theory bans, Black Studies programmes shuttering and DEI office closures are so nefarious and downright chilling. The people that know the history, the facts and the truth want it to go away; they know if the truth continued to come out, the rising tide of consciousness would wash away their sandcastles. The oppressors needed to continue to feed the coal-burning internal combustion engine of ignorance. The oppressors tried to protect this engine while softening the blow, one that is well-known to those in Black, Indigenous and racialized bodies, by invoking DEI, as opposed to confronting systemic anti-Black racism. However, the majority caught on that this was just a ruse. This reality is particularly damaging as true liberation of the Black oppressed was to achieve a level of humanism for all; for the oppressed to 'liberate themselves', they must also liberate their oppressors (Freire, 1970, p. 18).

Does anyone remember Florida's Trayvon Martin? London's Stephen Lawrence? Toronto's Raymond Lawrence? Probably not. With our society's collective memory of a goldfish – a deliberate conditioning that allows us to make the same mistakes of our past to benefit the few – we seem to think that anti-Black racism, and the soothing balm of DEI, started with George Floyd. The Rodney King Riots, the Yonge Street Rebellion, the rampant anti-Black racism in the United Kingdom (UK) during the 1990s, and the murders of Trayvon Martin, Michael Brown and many more Black people at the hands of (White) state violence are not isolated incidents but rather glaring examples of a systemic plague that has long afflicted Black communities worldwide. These events, each a flashpoint of racial injustice, collectively expose the brutal reality of police violence and institutional racism. The Rodney King Riots and Yonge Street Rebellion were explosive outcries against the unchecked brutality of law enforcement, while the murder of Stephen Lawrence in the UK laid bare the deep-seated institutional racism within the police force. The senseless killings of Trayvon Martin and Michael Brown further illuminated the persistent and deadly consequences of racial profiling.

These atrocities predate the BLM movement and the murder of George Floyd in 2020, yet they are the very foundation upon which BLM stands. They are the harrowing reminders of a long history of oppression and the urgent need for radical change. The BLM movement did not emerge in a vacuum; it is the culmination of decades of pain, resistance and the relentless fight for justice. These events are a testament to the systemic rot that BLM seeks to eradicate, and they underscore the imperative for a global reckoning with racial injustice. The time for complacency is over. The demand for equality and accountability is not just a call to action; it is a moral imperative.

Canada and the International Decade for People of African Descent: International Recognition, National Optics and the Limits of Multicultural Legality When Redistribution Is Off the Table

The annals of 'race relations' of the mid-to-late 20th century Canada highlight attempts to 'appease' and prevent social unrest, largely conceptualized as the 'American problem' of racism. 25 May 2020 destabilized White 'social cohesion' and Black assimilated docility predicated on the ideology, policy and legislation of Multiculturalism in 1971 and 1988. By 'White social cohesion', it goes to the idea that if everyone aims to fit the ideals of Whiteness (e.g. assimilate and be 'included' in dominant structures) we are living in a fair and equal society. Frances Henry and Effie Ginzberg (1985) argued that denying Black youth socioeconomic opportunities could lead to the destabilization of a Canadian false sense of 'racial' cohesion. They stated, 'We know from experiences of other countries such as Great Britain, that such feelings can lead to social unrest and disorder which no society can justify or endure' (Henry & Ginzberg, 1985, as cited in James, 2022, p. 358). Speaking on multiculturalism in 1984, Roy McMurtry, the Attorney General for the province of Ontario, opined on the disproportionate unemployment rates for non-White youths; 'if thousands of racial minority individuals in this country are given reason to believe that they face perpetual, widespread unemployment and second-class status because of the colour of their skin, very serious social unrest could result' (James, 2022, p. 358).

The policy-driven support of multiculturalism in 1971, which followed the official de-racialization of Canadian immigration policy in 1962, did not solve systemic anti-Black racism. Nor did the implementation of the Points System in 1967; the *Charter of Rights and Freedoms* of 1982; the *Multiculturalism Act* of 1988; or the *Anti-Racism Act* of 2017. These are all examples of Canadian race relations appeasement. It is clear that previous policies and legislations did not 'fix' the 'race problem' in Canada. They were merely neoliberal features of Canada's settler colonial system that maintains the illusion of systemic change, appealing to Black 'Excellence' and a *transnational habitus* of social mobility – the idea your skills and culture you bring from 'back home' will help you move up in Canadian society. It is also clear that Canada did not import racism from the US; it is all homegrown.

Prior to 25 May 2020, I argue that few institutions in Canada outwardly recognized the significant international support for Black empowerment and condemnation of the state's treatment of Black people. While the preamble of *The Scarborough Charter* and concrete actions to address anti-Black racism in post-secondary institutions, discussed in detail in Part II of this book, briefly highlights the historical, legal and policy frameworks that it is 'Responding' to, one may argue that most signatories are responding to the emotional cognitive dissonance of the events following 25 May 2020. The publication of the Report of the Working Group of Experts on People of African Descent (Working Group, 2017), following its mission to Canada in October 2016, clearly highlighted the historical and contemporary anti-Black racism embedded in Canadian institutions. Throughout the report, the Working Group (2017) highlighted a series of disparities and was 'deeply concerned by the structural racism that lies at the core of many Canadian institutions and the systemic anti-Black racism that continues to have a negative impact on the human rights situation of African Canadians' (p. 7). The Working Group (2017) provided several recommendations for the Government of Canada, including those related to education and credential attainment of Black youth in the elementary and secondary school levels. They recommended Canada 'implement a nationwide African Canadian education strategy to address the inordinately low educational attainment, high dropout rates, suspensions and expulsions experienced by African Canadian children and youth' (Working Group, 2017, p. 19) to support the work of the Charter.

The United Nations International Decade for People of African Descent (UNDPAD): Recognition Expands, Yet Precarity Persists

The UNDPAD came to be on 23 December 2013 (UN General Assembly, 2013). The main objectives of the UNDPAD (UN General Assembly, 2014) include:

> To promote respect, protection and fulfilment of all human rights and fundamental freedoms by people of African Descent, as recognized in the Universal Declaration of Human Rights;
>
> To promote a greater knowledge of and respect for the diverse heritage, culture and contribution of people of African descent to the development of societies;
>
> To adopt and strengthen national, regional and international legal frameworks according to the Durban Declaration and Programme of Action and the International Convention on the Elimination of All Forms of Racial Discrimination and to ensure their full and effective implementation. (p. 4)

The Durban Declaration and its Programme of Action, published in 2002, pushed for concrete initiatives and actions to repair the harms caused by enslavement of Black peoples, colonialism and historical human trafficking of Black bodies within, and from, the African continent (UN General Assembly, 2014).

The UNDPAD focuses on three main areas: Recognition, Justice and Development. Under Recognition, Black people have the right 'equality and non-discrimination' (UN General Assembly, 2014, p. 5). As it relates to Justice, the UNDPAD champions 'the adoption of special measures, such as affirmative action', as 'essential to alleviating and remedying disparities in the enjoyment of human rights and fundamental freedoms affecting people of African descent, protecting them from discrimination and overcoming persistent or structural disparities and de facto inequalities resulting from historical circumstances' (UN General Assembly, 2014, p. 8). The Education subcategory under Development encourages states to 'take measures to ensure that public and private education systems do not discriminate against or exclude children of African descent, and that they are protected from direct or indirect discrimination, negative stereotyping, stigmatization and violence from peers or teachers', and that competency and capacity building is needed for educators (UN General Assembly, 2014, p. 9). A key outcome of the UNDPAD was the establishment of the Permanent Forum on People of African Descent from the Resolution adopted by the General Assembly on 2 August 2021 (UN General Assembly, 2021). Ahmed Hussen, Canadian Minister of Housing and Diversity & Inclusion, participated in the first session of the Permanent Forum. He stated the Canadian government is in support of the Permanent Forum and the state will 'continue to build on our progress towards a more safe, inclusive and equitable Canada where no one is left behind' (Government of Canada, 2022, para. 5). While commendable, his statement reaffirmed the pacified nature of equity and inclusion as it reinforces the reified ideology of 'fairness' of political and socio-economic systems designed to marginalize and exclude.

I argue that many of the 'reforms' or Black-focused initiatives we witnessed in society post-25 May 2020, including the widespread support of DEI initiatives in Canadian Predominantly White Institutions (PWIs), were performative. I would go even further to say that these 'changes' were the result of Canadian, and broader Western, fears of unapologetic Blackness. These fears are the foundation of the Negro-Apocalypse I describe in this chapter; society needed to 'stop' the racial (re)awakening of Black Power in the 2020s, reignited in a new generation of oppressed peoples in response to highly publicized state violence. Again, this reality is rooted in the early twentieth-century Canadian fear of Black men violating the sanctity of White womanhood that contributed to the exclusion of Black settlement of Canadian provinces. What is interesting about this moment of time in the mid-2020s is how the rise of Black people in positions of power (albeit in DEI offices) incited this same visceral fear of violating the sanctity of PWIs and the mythical idea of 'meritocracy'. The idea that 'White-is-Right' contrasts with the assumption that 'Black-is-Bad' and therefore does not belong in Canadian/American/British boardrooms. This is similar to the twentieth-century ideal that Black people did not belong in Canada. Well, if we cannot keep them out of our country, we can keep them out of the halls of power. DEI, and its assimilative offshoots, was to work the same way that multiculturalism in Canada operated; to project an idea of tolerance, insofar as the Oppressed Other fit within the cultural and racial frameworks of (white) French and English Canadians. In under a decade in the 2020s, the apparent threat to the status quo was so great that the powers that be had to shut down the whole operation of DEI completely.

This small sample of historical events created the foundation for post-25 May 2020 ideologies about how to appeal to upwardly mobile, capitalist and neoliberal Black Canadian sensibilities. If the state supports superficial change, including an infusion of time-limited human and financial resources, kneeling photo-ops, support for 'equity' committees and working groups, petitions, pledges, virtual meetings, university programmes and the creation of entire equity and inclusion EDI-R offices with well-compensated tenured professors, for them, it is problem solved. Though changes might be tangible, ephemeral and superficial 'solutions' simply mask the foundational and root causes of systemic anti-Black racism. This tendency only serves to subsequently reinforce and perpetuate historical divisions and oppression. Analogous to his interrogation of neo-colonialism, Dr Kwame Nkrumah (1965) stated,

> neo-colonialism, like colonialism before it, postpones the facing of the social issues which will have to be faced by the fully developed sector of the world before the danger of world war can be eliminated or the problem of world poverty resolved. (p. xii)

I contend that while laudable, ambitious and needed, The Scarborough Charter does not adequately engage with the neo-colonial underpinnings of 'inclusive excellence' or 'Black excellence'. I need you to ask yourselves this question: when you encounter a DEI programme, what fear is it designed to calm, and whose power does it leave intact? Conversely, when you find a 'win', what did you have to give up?

Reflections on DEI and the Negro-Apocalypse

I was sitting in the audience of a talk with Too Black and Rasul A. Mowatt (2024), the authors of *Laundering Black Rage: The Washing of Black Death, People, Property and Profits*. Too Black was explaining the basic concept of laundering Black Rage; how the constructive and productive response to anti-Black systemic oppression is pacified and controlled by the institutions and the state. In his example, he used a rather simple but profound concept of the contradictions of someone who is trying to satisfy their hunger. I am paraphrasing, but the general concept goes like this:

> If you are hungry, what do you do? You go and buy food. But if you are living in poverty with no money, how do you get food? You ultimately have two choices: get sick and/or die from starvation, or steal food to survive. If you tell someone you're starving and they don't give you food or fix the systemic issues causing your hunger, but companies pledge to buy lunches from Black caterers, does that solve the problem? What if multinational corporations decide to hire more Black or non-White people to work as executives, are you no longer hungry? What if Black or non-White restaurant owners get more Michelin stars and are profiled in leading culinary publications, does that fix the core issue of one person's documented death from starvation?

This contradiction on hunger sat with me for a long time. With such a straightforward concept, it summarized the external and internal contradictions of my issues with DEI, and my role. I have profited from Black Death. Yes, there is no other way to articulate this reality with honesty and integrity. Without teenager Darnella Frazier's – now a Pulitzer Prize winner – 8:46 recording of George Floyd's murder, I would not have become Associate Vice-President. A lot of Black people would not have received their (well-earned and long-deserved) promotions. 'Buy Black' and Black businesses received the (well-earned and long-deserved) recognition and loans that have been historically denied. The reality of the diversity and plight of the Black existence in the West were finally 'seen' in schools, the workplace and in society. DEI, and 'woke', albeit around for decades in law and in historical literature, would not have risen to the consciousness of the mainstream public otherwise.

Yes, the general boredom of the pandemic lockdowns of 2020 gave this 8 minutes and 46 seconds the unrelenting attention that it rightfully deserved, but the police have killed Black people across Canada, the UK and the US since the beginning of formal policing. In fact, policing, particularly in the US, was built to control and patrol Black bodies during enslavement. Police and Black Death go hand in hand. Yes, our society has the collective memory of goldfish, but we – those that are in the DEI world or have benefitted since 2020 from a 'DEI' programme – cannot sit with a clear conscience and admit that if it was not for Darnella and George that we would be in the same position that we are now. Our hunger contradiction was satisfied by the death of someone else. I live with this reality as I wake up every morning grateful for the life that Black Death – whether it was George Floyd, or the millions of my kin on the bottom of the Atlantic Ocean, or buried on the grounds of Newton Plantation in Barbados – gave for me to be who I am. Yes, I am grateful and blessed, but it does not absolve the fact that my relationship with DEI is complex and challenging. Nor does this absolve the fact that without the reality of systemic anti-Black racism, I and other Black people would not have needed DEI to be successful. DEI is my hunger contradiction.

I have been in the DEI 'game' long before many people took the Implicit Association Test or received unconscious bias 'training' from a consultant with lived experience. I am a 'traditional' historian by training; however, as I mentioned, my scholarship and perspectives are shaped by the ethos and tenets of Black Studies. I work in systems, informed by communities, to produce knowledge that is accessible by these communities to support and promote actions for their use. I cannot control how these communities use this information or they how they feel about my role in the Establishment, but my goal is always to live with integrity. This is a challenge when I live with the contradiction of being within a capitalist system that is fundamentally designed to exploit the masses. What I find gets lost in these critiques of DEI, or the system, or colonialism, particularly by academics, is how in many ways we benefit from the system. Some, not all, of us have the platform to critique institutions that pay us. Some of us choose not to, and for those that do, it can be seen as a fundamental contradiction. I do not believe that it is hypocrisy, nor do I feel that it is not valued or important. I think the key is to admit that we live in this contradiction; that we acknowledge the space(s) that we inhabit may make us agents of White supremacy. However, as Too Black and Mowatt (2024) say, we can also have the ability to 'reverse launder'. That is, we can have the ability to use our positions in the capitalist ivory tower to, both literally and figuratively, fund and resource the collective movements that will fundamentally change the systems that we are in.

For me, in a very practical sense, it looks like this: I used, and continue to use, DEI as a vehicle to change, or what I call my shadow strategy. The 'D' in diversity has given me the opportunity to be hired as a 'token'. For some, this may seem like a negative, but for me, I saw it as an opportunity. In 2020 and 2021, if they were promoting Black people into executive positions to feed the contradiction of Black Death, I was going to jump into that role with both feet; not to placate Whiteness, but for my own agenda. I used the 'E' in equity as a tool to collaborate with like-minded others with our collective shadow strategies. On the outside, this may have appeared to appease the Establishment; an opportunity for Black people to come together and talk about our past wrongs and how we can come together and trauma bond. The reality? We were building long-lasting infrastructure and networks that were, and are, difficult to remove once the 'anti-woke' movement reappeared. Finally, I used the 'I' in inclusion as a façade of assimilation and integration. I did not, and do not, care to belong. I am a square peg trying to fit into a round hole; if you don't want me to fit in, I won't. However, I will learn everything I need to learn to know you and the game you are trying to play, inside and out. I will sit at tables that you thought I was just happy to be at, while also plotting, learning, engaging and reading the plays of a world I was never supposed to know existed. There is a reason that it was illegal for enslaved people to read or write. Knowledge is power. DEI gave me the opportunity to learn how the money and power are laundered and how it benefits the few. More importantly, it taught me how we have historically used DEI to appease and oppress. I decided it would not happen to me.

It hasn't.

Conclusion

This chapter named the pattern: the public revelation of anti-Black violence, the initial symbolic institutional embrace, the subsequent organized backlash and consolidation of the status quo. This pattern is all made possible by DEI, functioning as the key mediating technology. We also surfaced a counter-pattern: reverse-laundering, wherein Black leaders work to leverage their limited aperture to build infrastructure, archives and coalitions that persist after the spotlight fades. The lesson is not cynicism, it is strategy. Having established the cycle and the strategies that disrupt it, the next chapter turns to institutions – especially universities – and the Scarborough Charter movement. We will test whether 'inclusive excellence' and data-driven equity mechanisms put forth as hallmarks of this DEI movement can move from appeasement to accountable transformation in hiring, curriculum, evaluation and governance, or whether they reproduce the very neoliberal logics we have reviewed thus far.

References

Baldwin, J. (1993). *The fire next time*. Vintage Books.

Freire, P. (1970). *Pedagogy of the oppressed* (M. B. Ramos, Trans.). Herder and Herder. (Originally published in 1968).

Government of Canada. (2022, December 7). *Minister Hussen participates in the first session of the United Nations Permanent Forum on People of African Descent*. https://www.canada.ca/en/employment-social-development/news/2022/12/minister-hussen-participates-in-the-first-session-of-the-united-nations-permanent-forum-on-people-of-african-descent.html

Henry, F., & Ginzberg, E. (1985). *Who gets the work? A test of racial discrimination in employment*. Urban Alliance on Race Relations & The Social Planning Council of Metropolitan Toronto. https://urbanalliance.wordpress.com/wp-content/uploads/2012/05/who-gets-the-work.pdf

James, C. E. (2022). "We have to strive for the best" The high aspirations of Black Canadian Caribbean youth of the 1970s and 1980s. In M. A. Johnson & F. Aladejebi (Eds.), *Unsettling the great white north: Black Canadian history* (pp. 357–379). University of Toronto Press.

King, J. B. (2025). *King James Bible Online*. (Originally published in 1611). https://www.kingjamesbibleonline.org/

Nkrumah, K. (1965). *Neo-colonialism: The last stage of imperialism*. International Publishers.

Too, B., & Mowatt, R. A. (2024). *Laundering Black rage: The washing of Black death, people, property, and profits*. Routledge.

UN General Assembly. (2013). *Resolution 68/237: Proclamation of the international decade for people of African descent*. United Nations. https://docs.un.org/en/A/RES/68/237

UN General Assembly. (2014). *Resolution 69/16. Programme of activities for the implementation of the international decade for people of African descent*. United Nations. https://docs.un.org/en/A/RES/69/16

UN General Assembly. (2021). *Resolution 75/314: Establishment of the permanent forum of people of African descent*. United Nations. https://docs.un.org/en/A/RES/75/314

Working Group of Experts on People of African Descent [Working Group]. (2017). *Report of the working group of experts on people of African descent on its mission to Canada*. United Nations Human Rights Council. https://digitallibrary.un.org/record/1304262?ln=en&v=pdf

Chapter 5

DEI, Anti-Black Racism and the University's Response to the Negro-Apocalypse

Changes for Academia: Understanding White Supremacist Organizations and The Case of the Scarborough Charter

From Revelation to Response: How Universities Metabolized the 2020 Negro-Apocalypse

Chapter 4 named this moment the Negro-Apocalypse; a period when the routine precarity of Black life became visible to broader publics, followed almost immediately by institutional pacification (e.g. committees, pledges, cluster hires) and then a coordinated anti-DEI backlash. Universities, as producers and validators of knowledge and legitimacy, absorbed the crisis through symbolic gestures of inclusion while preserving decision rights, later consolidating hierarchy as political winds shifted. This chapter examines that cycle inside the academy; the organizational cultures that make appeasement predictable and the formal projects – most notably the Scarborough Charter – that promise transformation while remaining entangled with settler-colonial and neoliberal logics.

To understand why higher education so efficiently converts moral urgency into managerial process, we must treat White supremacy not only as extremist identity but also as an organizational common sense, a culture that prizes perfectionism, urgency, paternalism, power-hoarding and 'objectivity' as professional norms. These habits appear race-neutral yet reliably reproduce racial hierarchy. In the aftermath of 2020, they shaped which 'solutions' were thinkable and palatable (training sessions, dashboards, statements) and which remained unthinkable (redistributing authority, budgets and evaluation standards).

Unmasking DEI, 65–88

doi:10.1108/978-1-83708-356-520261005

The Scarborough Charter codified principles (Black Flourishing, Inclusive Excellence, Mutuality and Accountability) that many institutions embraced as a roadmap. Yet these principles can easily be enacted as appeasement DEI when 'inclusion' means assimilation into preexisting standards of 'excellence' and 'accountability' and is administrative rather than consequential, and 'mutuality' recruits Black communities into institutional priorities without shifting power. The Charter's guardrails matter, but without confronting governance, metrics and decision rights, outcomes skew towards recognition without redistribution.

Even within constrained regimes, actors can build shadow strategies, using temporary apertures to create infrastructures, archives, coalitions and funding channels that outlast cycles of backlash. This chapter provides a vocabulary for such work, including the concept of racial conduits, and tests these strategies against university practice.

White Supremacy Culture at Work: 'Professionalism' as a Politics of Power

What is White supremacy? It is quite interesting that most people could define this contentious phrase by describing the KKK, neo-Nazis and nativists, but what does it mean as it relates to systems, particularly organizations that we spend most of our working lives going in and out of? As I previously stated in this book, Frances Lee Ansley (1989) described White supremacy in this way:

> By 'White supremacy' I do not mean to allude only to the self-conscious racism of White supremacist hate groups. I refer instead to a political, economic and cultural system in which Whites overwhelmingly control power and material resources, conscious and unconscious ideas of White superiority and entitlement are widespread, and relations of White dominance and non-White subordination are daily re-enacted across a broad array of institutions and social settings. (p. 1024)

White supremacy is fundamentally about power, control and dominance. It is the means of oppressing the Other (non-Whites) through politics, culture, education and the status quo of day-to-day life. Yes, you can be non-White and adopt the ideology of White supremacy, or what I call being an *agent of White supremacy*. These agents of White supremacy, or as Dr King Jr. called them – White moderates – operate within the confines of DEI frameworks. Black skins with White masks that give the appearance of change through 'trainings' and representation in glass cliff positions, while maintaining dominant structures of control. It is the illusion of change in the hands of non-Whites, or 'allies', that allows for the consolidation of power in White supremacist organizations. Moving beyond the theory, what does this look like in practical terms within institutions?

The Organizational Habits That Make Appeasement DEI Predictable

Tema Okun's (2017, 2021) notes on White supremacy culture highlight organizational behaviours that perpetuate systemic inequities (see Appendix A). Perfectionism leads to a lack of appreciation for individual efforts, while a sense of urgency sacrifices inclusivity and thoughtful decision-making for quick wins. Defensiveness protects existing power structures rather than addressing racism, and prioritizing quantity over quality undermines meaningful relationships and democratic processes. The worship of the written word excludes non-written forms of communication, and the belief in only one right way stifles innovation. Paternalism concentrates decision-making power among a few, and either/or thinking limits problem-solving. Power hoarding prevents sharing power and embracing change, while fear of open conflict suppresses difficult conversations. Individualism and the belief in 'I'm the only one' hinder teamwork and delegation, and defining progress as bigger and more leads to unsustainable growth. Objectivity invalidates emotional experiences, and equating individual discomfort with systemic oppression minimizes the experiences of marginalized groups. Addressing these issues requires fostering inclusivity, collaboration and thoughtful decision-making to create a more equitable environment.

Taken in isolation and at face-value, these 15 behaviours do not seem to perpetuate a mainstream understanding of White supremacy. In no area does it say that 'White people burn crosses on the desks of Black people' or that 'White people fire Black people just because they are Black;' this does not refer to outright hostility and overt violence against non-Whites. Rather, Okun (2017, 2021) clearly identifies how insidious, pervasive and embedded White supremacy is in our institutions. It encompasses the 'acceptable' behaviours that define a 'traditional' or 'professional' organization. It is the 'normal' ways of doing business, such as teaching Black children to code-switch or have segmented identities and not bring their 'whole' or 'authentic' selves to work. It is what we implicitly and explicitly teach non-conforming employees on how to 'fit in' to a Western business or professional culture. Through appeasement DEI, and not system or culture change, we are asking (demanding) people to be inclusive of abusive behaviours. To be 'good' leaders, we are asking people to conform to dominant and hegemonic ways of perfectionism, individualism and power hoarding. Since this is what we are told is the best way for Western businesses, schools and organizations to function, we are forced to accept and adopt this neoliberal sense of being. If we question or challenge the status quo, people (particularly Black people) are told that their services are no longer welcome due to the fact they are not 'team players' or that they do not 'fit' the organizational culture. These behaviours do not constitute the foundations or frameworks of a healthy workplace. In reality, one could read these 15 behaviours and argue they are the characteristics of a *dysfunctional* organization. This is the truth; White supremacy does not benefit progress, nor does it benefit the well-being of all employees, irrespective of the intersections of their identities. The real conversation in DEI circles must be centred on the ways that Whiteness and White supremacy are detrimental to society, business, education and to White people as well.

Conforming to the Ideals of 'Professionalism' to Keep Non-Whites in Check Also Hurts White People

As Jonathan M. Metzl (2019) wrote in *Dying of Whiteness: How The Politics of Racial Resentment is Killing America's Heartland*, using a case study of a White Trump supporter, White people show a 'literal willingness to die for [their] place in this [White] hierarchy, rather than participate in a system that might put [them] on the same place as immigrants or racial minorities' (p. 4). He went on to say that 'Trump supporters were willing to put their own lives on the line in support of their political beliefs' (Metzl, 2019, p. 5). Scholars Joseph Mensah and Christopher J. Williams in *Boomerang Ethics: How Racism Affects Us All* (2017) wrote:

> We do not call for Whites to eschew racism just because they have some pity on, or compassion for, Blacks. Rather, our call is for Whites to do so also because racism is as wrong as it is at odds with their own self-interest in the long-run. (p. 9)

I argue, and have seen in different professional and academic roles, that these 15 behaviours only benefit the handful of (White) people at the top, those for whom that power and control is paramount to their identity. It, as Baldwin (1993) wrote, is a central characteristic of their Self; an identity built on lies and violence, which ultimately leaves them with deep senses of insecurity, knowing that they can be exposed for their mediocrity at any moment. People hate and fear most their deepest insecurities. Unfortunately, but not surprisingly, these behaviours are reflective of a neoliberal society where -isms like sexism, racism and classism maintain and perpetuate capitalist and individual greed. Paraphrasing and adapting the words of Eric Williams on the roots of Black enslavement and dehumanization in 2020s parlance, all we need to do is follow the money.

Shelby F. Lewis (1997) argues, 'Educational systems reflect the values and practices of the larger society. If the larger society is sexist, racist and based on economic, cultural and historical inequities, it is unrealistic to expect educational systems to be devoid of these inequities' (p. 42). Signatories of The Scarborough Charter (The Charter), and those tasked to design and implement strategies to confront anti-Black racism, must engage with the foundational paradigm of the Predominantly White institution (PWI) as an inherently anti-Black location. Canadian institutions must not only acknowledge that our institutions are predominantly White, but unpack the ways that anti-Black racism and Black exclusion have been, and continue to be, core to post-secondary institutions in Canada. This must move beyond the simple recognition of Black 'firsts' or what Debra Thompson (2022) refers to as the 'Only Ones'. Moreover, it cannot rest within the Land or Body Acknowledgements, or the removal of an institution's name or figurehead. Stakeholders of The Charter must lay bare and reckon with the settler colonial foundations of PWIs in Canada in order to affect the change that they profess to seek.

Predominantly White Institutions and Systemic Oppression at Play

PWIs have been defined in different ways by different scholars over time. Some scholars have defined them primarily through demographics, wherein PWIs are 'institutions of higher learning in which Whites have historically accounted for 50 percent or more of the student enrollment' or, because of 'diversity efforts' institutions in which 'Whites are by far still the most sizeable racial group' (Thacker & Freeman, 2021, p. 162). However, I agree with Griffith et al. (2017) who note that institutions do not have to have a numerical supremacy of White-identified students to be predominantly White. What defines a PWI, then, is an institution with a history of Black or non-White exclusion and by which 'non-White culture' is less represented (Griffith et al., 2017). These also 'tend to be contexts rife with race-related stressors such as seeing few other Black students in one's classes or on campus and experiencing discrimination' (Griffith et al., 2017, p. 116). Accordingly and most importantly, a PWI is rooted in the changing realities of settler colonialism and its impacts on pedagogy, policy and practice.

In *No Study Without Struggle: Confronting Settler Colonialism in Higher Education*, Leigh Patel (2021) argues that 'education has been crucial to the multifaceted project of settler colonialism' (p. x). This ontology is missing from The Charter: higher education in Canada is colonial, and by virtue, anti-Black. Any effort to reform, but not eliminate or destroy the sector, simply perpetuates colonial structures. Settler colonialism, as defined by Patrick Wolfe (2006), 'destroys to replace' (p. 388). Referring to Raphaël Lemkin, Wolfe (2006) expands on this definition:

> settler colonialism has both negative and positive dimensions. Negatively, it strives for the dissolution of native societies. Positively, it erects a new colonial society on the expropriated land base – as I put it, settler colonizers come to stay: invasion is a structure not an event. (p. 388)

Land, and the acquisition of or displacement of people from, is the organizing principle of settler colonialism. It facilitates the commodification of nature, along with the construction of racial hierarchies and dehumanization through its nihilistic classification and devaluation of people as a means of production. In PWIs, Patel (2021) argues that the 'settler colonial project first constructed colleges as places for the ministerial education of wealthy men, with strict focus on Greek, Latin, geometry, logic, ethics, and theology Settler colonialism'

(p. 56). Building on Paulo Freire's concept of the 'banking approach' to education, Patel (2021) contended that White 'privileged male students, were seen as vessels in which the culture of the colony should be sown, in essence advancing the project of knowledge for the purpose of domination and property accumulation' (p. 57). While education, and the legislated denial of formal/colonized education for Black people during enslavement in the Americas, was an accepted practice, this truism must be contextualized by the reality that this process was a tool to invoke conformity to the hegemonic power of the ruling elites for all peoples within a settler colonial state.

This understanding of settler colonialism as an active and persistent attempt to dispossess lands, cultures and bodies, is foundational learning when attempting to challenge, or navigate, PWIs and the implementation of The Charter recommendations. Patel (2021), referring to Historian Robin D. G. Kelley, argued that he 'does not see the university as an engine for social change, nor a place capable of loving the students that it actively dehumanizes through its research, its Eurocentric pedagogies and its investments in prison systems and planet-plundering industries' (p. 4). The Charter is asking, not demanding (and this distinction must remain clear), that PWIs change for the better good of society through the improving systems for Black students, faculty and staff. In *The History of Black Studies*, Abdul Alkalimat (2021) explores the creation of Black Studies, established formally in the 1960s with roots throughout the 20th century, responding to the deficit, difference and dependency theories of the supposed inferiority of Black people. Black Studies, to me, is fundamentally about understanding the historical, political and social anti-Black oppression of PWIs, and finding Black-focused ways in dismantling the system and building anew. The only way to advance Black 'excellence' is to, from the teachings of Fanon and Black Studies, 'blow the colonial world to smithereens', thereby demolish the 'colonist's sector, burying it deep within the earth or banishing it from the territory' (Fanon, 1963/2004, p. 6). I challenge that The Charter does not explicitly build on the tenets of Black Studies as a physical and epistemological site for intellectual history, social movements and Black academic profession (Alkalimat, 2021). Rather, as I argue in the following section, the Charter can become a function of appeasement DEI.

The Scarborough Charter's Principle Vs Practice: Who Decides and What Counts as 'Excellence'

I argue, like that of DEI more broadly, that the most benevolent outcome of the Scarborough Charter is pursuing a mirage of equity within an inequitable system. I contend that The Charter does just that for Black equity, enabling this mirage within an inequitable system that will only continue to support Black elites that adopt and achieve metrics of Eurocentric understandings of 'excellence'. Measures of 'excellence' within a PWI, however, are crucial miscalculations of change, whether they are adopted as 'inclusive' measures of excellence or not. It effectively becomes an assimilative practice. The key discussion here centres on the predilection of The Charter's seemingly benevolent utilization of the term *Black Excellence*. Gosine (2019) highlights the fundamental issue, as Black Excellence:

> is actually an elitist concept that veils and enables systemic racism and resultant inequalities. Embedded in the meritocratic idea of 'excellence' is the belief that equality of opportunity flourishes, and understanding that, in turn, underpins an ostensible colour-blind or 'treat everyone the same' philosophy for creating an equitable society. (p. 254)

This, like arguments for DEI, disguises a class-based and power analysis of our historical understandings of Black liberation and the ways that Black people navigate White supremacist ideologies of heteronormative and 'civilized' ways of being.

While The Charter is necessary and signals needed 'guardrails' for institutional and interpersonal change for Black stakeholders (faculty, staff, and students) in PWIs in Canada, I argue that higher education in Canada has been, and continues to be, inherently oppressive and exclusionary. I deliberately use the term 'stakeholder' as a reference and acknowledgement that PWIs in Canada are functions of the neoliberal capitalist and settler colonial system. As paying consumers, Black students 'purchase' a colonial education and its by-product of employment in the capitalist system. Black faculty and staff are agents of the state; inadvertently cogs in the machine receiving compensation for their labour with varying levels of degrees (literal and figurative) of precarious employment and colonial vestiges of prestige. Meanwhile, as Rinaldo Walcott (2021) states, all Black people, in this case, stakeholders must operate knowing their bodies and existences as property. As is commonly understood, racism is capitalism and capitalism is racism. This foundational understanding of the positioning of Black people as maligned bodies in search of Eurocentric validation is key in understanding the strengths and limitations of The Charter. I challenge those of us of darker skin tones to understand how these systems work and create 'shadow strategies' for change, or we will simply adopt Whiteness and perpetuate exclusion of less-resourced Black communities as agents of White supremacy, just as the system expects us to.

The Charter, by way of its underpinnings of the appeasement and assimilation narratives of inclusion into PWIs, reinforces settler colonial exclusionary paradigms. In this way, The Charter, as Frantz Fanon (1963/2004) acutely determined, reinforces the belief that 'the colonized man is an envious man' (p. 5). I do not use this term lightly. Upon close reading of The Charter, particularly as it is juxtaposed to the historical and political manifestations of Black Studies, it asks (not demands) for Black people to be measured by the analogous metrics of success ('excellence') and to be included and valued within settler colonial structures. Higher education in Canada and across the Black Atlantic is a product and ideological representation of settler colonialism. While this approach may not be palatable to university administrators, this recognition allows for a greater understanding of the limits of The Charter and a level of humility-driven introspection of its structural and ideological contradictions. In the ethos of Fanon, one may argue that The Charter's unstated function is to create a generation of academic Black skin, White masks.

Upon close reading of the Scarborough Charter, it is clear this document is comprehensive and well-constructed. It is manageable, actionable and clearly directs institutions for tangible outcomes and change. While detailed, it is not restrictive, allowing for interpretation and regional, geographical and logistical adaptions for respective institutions of differing budgets, compositions and stakeholders. It is well-needed and will benefit PWIs across Canada. That being said, we must first engage with, and understand with a critical lens, the document itself. Many institutions were quick to sign The Charter as it did not, nor was it meant to, dictate overarching or (needed) disruptive change in institutions. It is driven by the principles of collective impact and targeted universalism, within which the 'target' is Black stakeholders, and the 'impacts' will catalyze structural changes to support all faculty, staff and students. The Charter is framed by four key principles, upon which post-secondary institutions can build their own respective action plans to confront anti-Black racism. The key principles include *Black Flourishing*, *Inclusive Excellence*, *Mutuality* and *Accountability* (Blackett et al., 2021).

Governance, Data and the Limits of Accountability: Why Boards, Senates and Budget Rules Matter More Than Slogans

Through *Black Flourishing*, schools should enable the 'fulsome realization of human potential and thriving', tasking PWIs to remove 'structural barriers' to advance 'innovative research, critical thinking and engaged dissemination of knowledge that foster substantive equality, human dignity and sustainability' (Blackett et al., 2021, p. 9). There are a number of principles to follow under Black Flourishing. As it relates to governance, PWIs are to ensure 'leadership on equity' that 'permeates governance structures across all university and college levels' (Blackett et al., 2021, p. 11). The focus on governance also includes incorporating processes that include non-Black PWI stakeholders to work with Black faculty, staff and student in 'achieving equity' (Blackett et al., 2021, p. 11).

The definition of *Inclusive Excellence* creates a paradigm of two exclusionary and misappropriated terms (both inclusion and excellence). This second principle argues that 'equitable inclusion is critical to excellence', as 'excellence' allows for innovation, education and proactivity to foster 'fundamental questioning through rigorous, respectful engagements across difference' and 'enable societal change' (Blackett et al., 2021, p. 9). Key activities under the principle include race-based disaggregated data collection to 'provide demographic knowledge of Black faculty, staff and students' in PWIs, and to increase Black student stakeholder representation through recruitment (Blackett et al., 2021, p. 12). The fundamental concern with this principle, and with Section 2.1.1 for Black recruitment, is that PWIs remain tied to Eurocentric ontologies of 'inclusion' and 'excellence', concepts that continue to force non-White bodies and epistemologies to 'fit in' dominant settler colonial structures, spaces and pedagogies. The idea that 'equitable inclusion' is possible within a PWI is a fallacy; the hierarchal, bureaucratic, settler colonial foundations of these institutions enforce Black homogeneity, conflicting epistemologies and assessments of 'excellence' that may differ from traditional definitions of 'excellence' in academia that induce conformity to standards of Whiteness. If not, they will either fail their courses or will not earn tenure. This principle should move away from the idea of inclusion and excellence, resting instead within an assessment of what is useful and impactful for domestic and global Black communities.

Mutuality refers to the 'positive, interactive relationship with Black communities', which includes the special role universities and colleges can assume in Black community economic development, notably as anchor institutions and local employers' (Blackett et al., 2021, p. 9). Section 3.3 focuses on teaching and learning, and states that PWIs should construct K-12 and post-secondary outreach programmes and adopt 'harassment-free' classrooms where 'rigorous study can occur' (Blackett et al., 2021, p. 14). Again, this is laudable, particularly as institutions focus on creating transitional year programmes for Black youth, and engage domestically and internationally with Black youth. However, we must proceed with caution of the power dynamics of reciprocity. Without a power-based analysis, The Charter is only promoting and advocating for hegemonic power where Black youth should want to be included in a PWI, whether it be academically or financially. This principle must first address the settler colonial trust deficit by which Black communities have been, and continue to be, exploited, particularly Black international students, to feed the higher education industrial complex.

The fourth principle, Accountability, outlines that PWIs 'must move beyond mere representation and take responsibility for supporting fulsome, transformative inclusion across university and college structures, policies and procedures', and 'includes acknowledging, respecting, and acting responsively in the face of Black life, in its full complexity and intersectionality' (Blackett et al., 2021, p. 9). Their 'respective Boards, communities and other stakeholders' will effectively hold PWIs accountable – 'answerable' – for deliverables (Blackett et al., 2021, p. 9). Accountability, too, as a word and concept, has been misappropriated. Mariame Kaba and Shira Hassan (2019) argue:

> The word 'accountability' is thrown around liberally, but is very poorly understood. There is no way to 'hold people accountable'. People can only 'take accountability'. Accountability is a continuous, active, and voluntary process of being responsible to yourself and those around you for your choices and the consequences of your choices. (p. 78)

Moreover, 'unlike punishment, it is something that we do rather than something that is done to us' (Kaba & Hassan, 2019, p. 78). The authors state that individuals and institutions must 'expect consequences for actions that we take, that we take responsibility for harms that we have done, that we understand the impact(s) of those harms, and, finally, that we focus on repairing them' (Kaba & Hassan, 2019, p. 78). In my experience from working in PWIs, the Charter is flawed as institutions rarely hold themselves accountable; they attempt to minimize the impacts of harms and refuse to engage in meaningful repair.

The Charter, and the vast majority of university policies, have clear lines for structural change for most Senate and Board configurations, governance bodies and overall governance at their institutions. Moreover, most stakeholders, irrespective of their pigmentation, lack a clear understanding of how governance bodies function, nor do they truly understand the nature of their oppression by these bodies. A tenured professor, or under Section 4.1.2., a 'senior administrator, wherever possible reporting to the university or college president or principal' (Blackett et al., 2021, p. 15) may lead the development and implementation of a confronting anti-Black racism action plan. However, this is in direct tension with the fact that most academic admissions or policy changes must receive Senate and Board approval. If the president approves but governance bodies are not aligned, efforts become a futile exercise of performative impotence. Governance bodies must first acknowledge how they have, and continue to, perpetuate anti-Black racism. This must happen not through statements, but tangible and transparent audits of decision-making processes, Board composition, the purpose of governance bodies and plain language articulation of meeting minutes targeted specifically to Black stakeholders. Specific action plans to confront anti-Black racism in governing bodies themselves must follow. Through an anti-settler colonial audit, I argue that it may, or will, be discovered that accountability is not the issue, but the nature of PWI governance itself. As outlined by Kaba and Hassan (2019), this is the fox guarding the hen house; until governance bodies outline the consequences of their role in perpetuating anti-Black racism, the Charter will remain ineffective.

A Way Forward: Confronting Anti-Black Racism in PWIs

Many institutions have adopted what Philip S. S. Howard (2019) termed the "good' White leader' (p. 233), reinforcing the hierarchal ineptitude of 'White saviourism' to assuage guilt. Further, this distinction constructs 'good' versus 'bad' White people, and by extension, 'good' and 'bad' institutions. PWIs rushed to create equity offices, leads or units, rooted in theory but absent of *praxis*. Howard (2019) argued this was done:

> to the extent that White people seek to construct a 'good' White identity, they will most often be involved in superficial forms of racial equity work where they 'either get their needs met' (rewards, accolades, immediate results) or do not have to do much work (no risk-taking, little complexity). (p. 221)

Along these lines, Howard (2019) discusses *interest convergence*, which I argue is a key feature of the Negro-Apocalypse climate. Howard (2019) roots this theory in the 'critical race theory tenet positing that ostensible racial equity gains are seldom significantly influenced by White concern of racial injustice…but rather are made where there is an apparent convergence with the interests of White people' (p. 221). Howard (2019), speaking directly to Black interlopers in PWIs, highlights racial fortuity, or 'the tactic of taking intentional advantage of interest convergences', and the ways this process can lead to the effective means to 'advance racial justice' (p. 233). The 'interest', for many Canadian institutions, was, and is, rooted in collective (White) guilt, saviourism, denial and twenty-first-century social media public relations. Moreover, it is rooted in what I have termed the *myth of the Underground Railroad*; the historically inaccurate moral suasion argument that positions Canada as 'better' than the United States (US) as it relates to its treatment of Black peoples. However, the reluctance to engage in the true deconstruction of White supremacist and settler colonial institutions, reinforced the performative nature of their activities, and set them on the course of (designed and deliberate) failure.

Howard (2019), among other scholars and activists, have highlighted several areas for change. The author implores leaders and, by extension, institutions, to learn from histories of Black resistance and agency. Embedded in its preamble, Charter signatories should be aware of the historical, political and social forces that facilitated the creation of this document. I contend that signatories must also be aware of historical and contemporary Black-led decolonization and liberation movements. Signatories should embody the spirit of the Militant Millennial, an ethos of Black liberation and resistance formed during the period of enslavement and rebellion in the Americas (Taylor, 2022). They must learn the, at times unpalatable, lessons of Fanon, Laws, Shadd, Augustine, Roach, Davis, Shakur and particularly the lessons of the young Black resistance movement at Sir George Williams in 1969. Most notably, signatories must be aware of the fallout that ensues when those, particularly Black women, dare to challenge and oppose the neoliberal ideologies of White hegemony.

We do not need to reinvent the wheel, nor construct complex solutions; if we adopt Afro-centric principles, such as *Sankofa*, we can succeed. *Sankofa*, for me, is the premise of this book and my *modus operandi* as I navigate and challenge PWIs. It is about learning from the lessons of my ancestors on how they were able to survive the horrors of enslavement, colonization and anti-Black racism. On top of that, *Sankofa* is about understanding my *Self*, not just within a space of anti-Blackness, but of love and humanity. It is about understanding my own goals in life of realizing my full potential as a human being. That is my desired outcome, and '*looking back, to go forward*' has taught me that the road map to achieve this is in plain sight in written and oral histories, but also Black-centred ways of being. Black implementers of The Charter must clearly articulate their desired outcome, to themselves and to their communities, whether they intend to work to dismantle anti-Black racism, or strive to increase representation. Regardless of their intentions, both should be clear in stating their goals and neither should obfuscate language to mislead stakeholders.

Converting Symbolic Space Into Durable Gains: Build What Cannot Be Quietly Reversed

PWIs must be cognizant of improving the lived experiences of those currently within oppressive structures. I question the efficacy of 'equity' as a means to an end within fundamentally inequitable PWI systems. Howard (2019) clearly defines racial equity as 'any institutional equity venture undertaken where race is named as a salient (though not necessarily exclusive) consideration' (p. 213). I argue that the term *racial equity* is used to encourage equity within inequitable systems, whereas terms such as liberation, justice or anti-racism actively reflect systems change. People and programmes rarely aim to disrupt the 'system' or liberate those who have been subjugated by it, leaning more towards equity, as the former can destabilize their positions in the institutions (e.g. losing their jobs). The caution I apply here, echoing Howard's warning, is that these efforts must not reinforce nor perpetuate the neo-colonial fabrication of Black skin, White masks as agents of White supremacy. The Charter is rooted in the neoliberal foundations of PWI oppression. Racial equity, in its current form, will simply produce a 'Talented Tenth' of Black oppressors that, in many cases, may have been chosen by the PWI to assuage guilt and perform containment. Black people, as Howard (2019) states, must have agency, which is 'understood at the level of the group, referring to Africans'/Black people's prerogative to evaluate matters in terms of their liberation… and to choose their own terms for collaborating with other groups' (p. 215).

Further key lessons from Howard (2019) include the reality that Black people cannot become the figurative and literal 'wall' to challenge all forms of institutional and interpersonal anti-Black racism. The Charter is deliberately non-prescriptive; however, objectives and key performance metrics must be clearly outlined, with defined accountability. The Charter does state the same, but enforcement is paramount. Howard (2019) continues stating that 'Black embodied knowledge' is a powerful resource (p. 237). I contend that, as does Grace Mathieson (2002), those engaged in this work must apply Black feminist theoretical frameworks. With their focus on amplifying voices, as well as reflexive and humanizing *praxis*, these frameworks will allow Black people in this work to 'affirm the resistance power that comes from asserting our humanity and refusing to be negated', and not 'underestimate the importance of Black resistance power' (Howard, 2019, p. 237).

Informed by my experiences as the Associate Vice President of Equity, Diversity, Inclusion and Anti-Racism (EDI-R), and in other anti-racism and equity roles in large, bureaucratic, and publicly-funded institutions, including the Government of Ontario, I contend that there are key strategies to successfully navigate, survive and thrive within PWIs and utilize The Charter on our own terms. For Black martyrs of The Charter, the most aspirational outcome is a Pyrrhic victory – losing everything for marginal or fleeting gains. In many cases for Black people, it means jeopardizing our mental and/or physical health in order to make incremental change. I contend that we must engage with truths and reconcile our professional and personal Self(s) with the ever-changing myth of success embedded in colonial and neo-colonial systems. We can be anti-colonial in our thoughts, words and deeds. I argue that within a global capitalist society founded on oppressive structures such as the human trafficking of Black bodies, resource extraction, colonialism and patriarchy, our goal is to survive (and thrive) within this White supremacist structure. If the global pandemic(s) of 2020 has taught us anything, we as leaders in this EDI-R space must recognize that only a select few hold true power, and we must target this few. The paradigm is key. As students and scholars in this space, this is not an intellectual or theoretical exercise. The ontological questions we ask, the epistemological resources we produce and consume, and the visions we shape are key in interrogating the kind of society we truly want. Most importantly, it allows us to 're-think' and 're-visit' whether the tools of DEI, and the 'allies' that wield them, are what we truly need. I believe that we need to continually rethink and re-evaluate the spaces that we are in – political, social and physical – and learn from our diverse histories of liberation to create new and effective means for change. One of our gifts as Black people is our ability to shift with changing tides of the Atlantic. In the DEI space, it is about us looking deep within ourselves and applying our intrinsic liberation strategies into everyday practice.

Racial Conduits and Anti-Racist Leaders

I argue that non-Black people within PWIs should work as *racial conduits*. The racial conduit framework, a term I have coined (Taylor, 2020a), positions (the use/denial of) power as a key function of White supremacy (Taylor, 2020b). The racial conduit centres 'power' as a tool that will either oppress or emancipate. A racial conduit is similar to what is commonly known as an 'anti-racist leader', but with one key caveat. The racial conduit, like the anti-racist leader, navigates between managerial and confrontational (Farrah, 2020) positions of challenging White supremacy; however, it distinctly forces the individual to acknowledge and reconcile how they benefit from the power and violence of White supremacy with their desire for institutional and societal change. Most anti-racist leaders do not necessarily centre their Self as beneficial to White supremacist organizations, and at times maintain a position of 'White saviourism'. The uncritical acceptance of systemic racism, and the power and violence embedded in all of our institutions, is a barrier that most White moderates refuse to acknowledge, let alone challenge. While beneficial and needed in PWIs and organizations, an anti-racist leader may be perceived to be static in their approach without flexibility of using their power to 'get out of the way' to allow change to happen without their direction. An individual can, and should, be both a racial conduit and an anti-racist leader.

The key behaviours of a racial conduit include understanding and accepting one's positionality and how one is perceived. In other words, individuals must learn and accept the histories and realities of White supremacy, and how one benefits in the present. A core knowledge of systems thinking is paramount. Actors must engage with an intersectional understanding of individual, situational and institutional power. At its core, a racial conduit is an individual who recognizes, identifies and accepts White supremacy as the key organizing principle of society, their spheres of influence and their own existence. Whiteness must be interrogated as an absolute truth by acknowledging the realities of White mediocrity, the related false sense of achievement and being and the nature of fabricated superiority, as well as their own relations with these realities. This recognition is crucial for understanding the pervasive nature of systemic racial violence and its impact on all aspects of life. Racial conduits should utilize their (individual, situational and institutional) power to create space for Black self-empowerment within systems. Upon building this foundation, racial conduits must give up their (individual, situational and institutional) power once Black communities are embedded as autonomous agents within systems, for either their maintenance or destruction. The racial conduit subsequently facilitates the removal of racist systemic barriers and creates space for the subaltern. Non-Black signatories of The Charter, and I would argue, many of those Black stakeholders that are not actively interested in dismantling the oppressive neoliberal PWI systems, should bare minimum ascribe to the position of the racial conduit. For more details about the characteristics of a racial conduit or anti-racist leader, refer to Appendix B of this chapter.

Along with being a racial conduit, here are four quick strategies of what you can do to maximize the full weight of interest convergence to your own benefit: 'Create Shadow Strategies', 'Know Thy Foe', 'You are on Your Own' and 'Cleary Defined Time Limit and Exit Strategy'.

Create Shadow Strategies

The Charter does well in giving space for liberal interpretations with its guardrails. Black implementers can, and should, become Black interlopers; learn how to use this Negro-Apocalypse to one's advantage to push (hidden) agendas that may not necessarily be palatable to the growing cacophony of anti-Black White moderates.

> Example: As a faculty member, if you are given a research budget (and it fits within policy and legal frameworks), make sure you hire Black research assistants that will support research that impacts Black communities. This does not necessarily mean doing 'Black research', which may seem too 'radical' for the PWI elites, but developing technologies and producing knowledge that will have exponential impacts on Black communities. We call this 'reverse money laundering'.

Know Thy Foe

Take to heart Dr King Jr.'s (1963) lesson on White moderates:

> I have almost reached the regrettable conclusion that the Negro's great stumbling block in his stride toward freedom is not the White Citizen's Counciler (sic) or the Ku Klux Klanner, but the White moderate, who is more devoted to 'order' than to justice; who prefers a negative peace which is the absence of tension to a positive peace which is the presence of justice; who constantly says: 'I agree with you in the goal you seek, but I cannot agree with your methods of direct action'. (para. 19)

The premise of the racial conduit is based on my reflections of the Radical Dr King Jr., whom I benevolently refer to as the santa-clausified 'Acceptable Negro'. Through a close reading of his managerial rhetoric, Dr King Jr. warned us of the limitations of the 'ally' and directed us towards the path of the racial conduit. As Dr King Jr. wrote on 16 April 1963, the 'White moderate' (para. 20) – an individual that works within our institutions, upholding laws, regulations, policies and order – is our greatest threat to racial equity and social justice. The danger we face is that many of these 'White moderates' are unaware of the fact they are actively maintaining the White supremacist status quo. They are oblivious to their positionality and power, and by following and enforcing 'rules', they are perpetuating anti-Black racism. A prime example is an educator who does not challenge the homogeneity of curricula within PWIs, the dearth of Black faculty on campus or the ideals of meritocracy, among others.

> Example: Always be cautious of the 'well-meaning' colleague that will shed a tear in a DEI session. The one that will say that they really want to make change, and for you to always reach out if you need support. Then when you present them with impactful measures, they come back to you with a very long email explaining why they cannot, or will not, do anything. Most of the time it is excuses around budget, capacity or one of my favourites – 'what about-isms' – how will other groups be impacted if we just focus on Black people. Do not put your trust in these White moderates that just want to maintain the status quo.

You Are On Your Own

The benefit of The Charter is that it creates, in the words of Benedict Anderson (1983), an imagined community of like-minded people invested in confronting anti-Black racism. However, it does not mitigate the presence of the debilitating reality and isolation of the 'only one' on campuses. Moreover, it does not alleviate the burden of Black implementers/interlopers in 'DEI' positions that face derision from those wanting to uphold colonial systems (White stakeholders), those at the helm of maintaining colonial systems (administration and governance bodies) and those that do not believe The Charter goes far enough (Black stakeholders). Ultimately, this is thankless work, and one must be prepared to live with a level of isolated grief and internalized trauma.

> Example: Going back to the Okun's principles of White supremacy culture, particularly those of individualism and fear, in a neoliberal society that is predicated on a scarcity mindset (e.g. publicly funded post-secondary institutions), people are in it for themselves. Whether they are Black, White, or Purple, there are many individuals that say one thing but mean the other. They might say that they are in their jobs for the public good, but ultimately they are only concerned about themselves: their own mortgages, their own pensions, and their own career progression. They are worried that if they put the collective above themselves, they may lose everything in a Pyrrhic Victory. Always remember that.

Clearly Defined Time Limit and Exit Strategy

It is not a failure to know when it is time to end your relationship with The Charter and confronting anti-Black racism. Black people have been engaged in this battle to (re)humanize our existence for centuries; it is okay to pass the baton to someone else when it is time. This work is psychologically and physically dangerous and there is resistance in rest. That being said, it is necessary to have clearly defined succession plans and foundations outlined so the next person involved does not fall into the 'Ferris wheel' trap of White supremacist collective amnesia.

> Example: Rest is resistance.

Reparations as Reconciliation: Locating Campus Change Within Broader Reparatory Frameworks

> the objective of reparations is not to punish or penalize the offender, but to establish conditions for a just, reconciled future. Reparation is not an action of confrontation, but a search for unity; that is, the aim is repairing a damaged relationship. (Beckles, 2013, p. 17)

This book holds that the roots of anti-Black racism lie in the dehumanization of Black bodies through the Transatlantic Slave Trade, the period of enslavement throughout the Black Atlantic and colonization. I can write pages of notes and actions on how to be a racial conduit or an anti-racist leader, what Black-first *praxis* looks like, the failures and misrepresentations of DEI. These pages, however, mean nothing without the acceptance of one key fact: the core facilitator of anti-Black racism is the continued dehumanization of Black people across the diaspora. Without this acceptance, there is no hope for us to move forward and repair the damaged relationship. So how does one repair this relationship? Yes, we as a society must (un)learn centuries of (mis)representations of Blackness and Black bodies. Yes, we must promote a decolonial (remove Eurocentric ways of learning) approach to education and be anti-colonial (fight against) all forms oppression. These are all needed approaches as we move forward in the liberation of Black peoples across the Black Atlantic, as we revisit Black-first modes of liberation and eschew the appeasement politics of DEI. The fight for reparations is one key direction that we must follow.

In 1928, the Permanent Court of International Justice (the predecessor of the International Court of Justice) outlined that 'the essential principle contained in the actual notion of an illegal act is that reparation must, as far as possible, wipe out all the consequences of the illegal act and re-establish the situation which would, in all probability, have existed if that act had not been committed' (Beckles, 2013, p. 13). Beckles (2013) defines reparations as 'the underlying principle within international law is that redress for human injustices, including crimes against humanity, is possible', and 'international law is explicit' that 'reparations must be paid in cases of proven crimes against humanity' (Beckles, 2013, p. 13, 17). The dehumanization of Black bodies was, and *is*, a crime against humanity. Moreover, as Beckles (2013) has researched extensively, the trading in Black bodies was an illegal act. In a society based on law and order, in a society that has criminalized Blackness and Black bodies, it may be jarring to some to read how enslavement was morally, ethically and legally wrong. Alongside North American genocide of Indigenous peoples and broken treaties, the economies and wealth of the United Kingdom (UK) and the US might as well have been the product of present-day state-sponsored money laundering or drug trafficking. This has been acknowledged in the university context in different ways. For example, in 2019, the University of Glasgow was required 'to pay £20m in reparations to atone for its historical links to the transatlantic slave trade in what the University of West Indies has described as a "bold, historic" move' (Carrell, 2019, para. 1). The truth and reconciliation of its past created a space to understand that:

> Glasgow University played a key role in the abolitionist campaign of the era but until recently Scotland's profiteering from slavery, including from tobacco and cotton plantations, was largely ignored. One of its former rectors was Robert Cunninghame Graham, who spent two decades making his fortune as a plantation owner and slaver. (Carrell, 2019, para. 7)

On a grander scale, we need to compare the leadership of Barbados' Prime Minister Mia Mottley in pushing for reparations today with the Black Panther Party (BPP) in the mid-20th century. Some conservatives might find this comparison controversial, but we can see similarities by looking at Caribbean Community's (CARICOM's) 10-Point Reparation Plan and the BPP's 10-Point Programme (see Appendix C). The CARICOM Reparations Justice Programme (CRJP) argued that '[European] governments, furthermore, served as the primary agencies through which slave based enrichment took place, and as national custodians of criminally accumulated wealth' (Caricom Reparations Commission [CRC], 2025, para. 2). Caribbean leaders set up the CRC in 2014 'with a mandate to prepare the case for reparatory justice for the region's indigenous and African descendant communities who are the victims of Crimes against Humanity (CAH) in the forms of genocide, slavery, slave trading and racial apartheid' (CRC, 2025, para. 1). Enslaved people and their descendants 'have a legal right to reparatory justice, and that those who committed these crimes, and who have been enriched by the proceeds of these crimes, have a reparatory case to answer' (CRC, 2025, para. 1).

Reparations, Not Just Representation: Moving From Inclusion to Repair

The 10-Point Reparation Plan includes actions like a full formal apology, repatriation, Indigenous Peoples Development Programme, cultural institutions, illiteracy eradication, African Knowledge Programme, psychological rehabilitation, technology transfer and debt cancellation (CRC, 2025). A key point is the focus on illiteracy eradication (Taylor, 2020a). Education, as is outlined in this book is key for moving forward to support Black liberation. The CRJP (CARICOM, 2014) states:

> Some 70 percent of [B]lacks in British colonies were functionally illiterate in the 1960s when nation states began to appear ... [W]idespread illiteracy has subverted the development efforts of these nation states and represents a drag upon social and economic advancement. Caribbean governments allocate more than 70 percent of public expenditure to health and education in an effort to uproot the legacies of slavery and colonization (Point 6).

This is a clear stance for justice through Black Power and Black-first *praxis*. As Kwame Ture (formerly Stokely Carmichael) and Ture and Hamilton (1967) note, 'We must not apologize for the existence of this form of group power' (p. 48). Ture and Hamilton (1967) argue that '[B]lack people have not suffered as individuals but as members of a group; therefore, their liberation lies in group action' (p. 54). Liberation and freedom, as shown by the 10-Point Reparation Plan and predicted by Ture and Hamilton in the 1960s, mean ending the 'dependent colonial status that has been inflicted upon it' (Ture & Hamilton, 1967, p. 55). The CRJP's call for reparations challenges the idea that 'colonial subjects have their political [and economic] decisions made for them by the colonial masters', underscoring the reality that 'politically, decisions which affect [B]lack lives have always been made by White people – the "White power structure"' (Ture & Hamilton, 1967, p. 6). Through the CRC and CRJP, Caribbean leaders like Prime Minister Mottley embody Black Power principles and confront White supremacy. They demand reparations in legal, social, psychological and economic forms.

This mirrors the BPP's focus on the damage caused by enslavement and the need for reparations, as outlined in their 10 Points on 15 May 1967. In volume 1, issue 2 of 'The Black Panther: Black Community News Service', the Black Panther published a set of what they believed was necessary for the Black community. It began by stating (see the appendix for the full list):

> To those poor souls who don't know Black History, the beliefs and desires of the Black Panther Party for Self Defense may seem unreasonable. To Black people, the Ten Points covered are absolutely essential to survival. We have listened to the riot of producing words 'these things take time' for 400 years. The Black Panther Party knows what Black people want and need. Black unity and self defense will make these demands a reality. (Black Panther Party, 1967, p. 3)

Prime Minister Mottley's leadership, along with that of other Black leaders across the diaspora, highlights the ongoing struggle for reparatory justice and Black liberation, particularly in juxtaposition with BPP's activism in the 1960s–1980s. Despite almost half of a century between their publication, both the CARICOM 10-Point Reparation Plan and the BPP's 10 Point Programme emphasize the need for systemic change and the importance of addressing historical injustices. The CRJP's focus on reparations for crimes against humanity committed during enslavement and colonization aligns with the BPP's call for freedom, employment, housing, education and an end to police brutality.

Kwame Ture's emphasis on group power and collective action underscores the necessity of a united front in the fight for justice. The CRJP's challenge to the White power structure and demand for reparations reflects the BPP's principles of self-defence and empowerment. The focus on illiteracy eradication and education in the 10-Point Reparation Plan mirrors the BPP's call for education that exposes the true nature of American society and teaches Black history. The comparison reveals that the fight for reparatory justice and Black liberation is a continuous effort that requires confronting systemic racism and advocating for meaningful change. Prime Minister Mottley's leadership in the Caribbean and the BPP's activism in the United States both represent significant steps towards achieving these goals.

In a way, and to make it more palatable to the masses, we can look at reparations through the DEI framework. The call for reparations and the challenge to the White power structure reflect a commitment to addressing systemic inequalities. Equity involves creating fair opportunities and outcomes for marginalized groups, and the text advocates for reparatory justice as a means to achieve this. The demand for reparations in legal, social, psychological and economic forms aligns with the principle of equity, recognizing the need to redistribute resources to rectify historical injustices and support the development and empowerment of Black communities. The CRJP and the BPP promote the true valuing of non-Eurocentric perspectives (i.e. diversity) and commitments to true system change (i.e. inclusion). Reparation frameworks move away from appeasement DEI. The emphasis on group action and collective liberation promotes an inclusive approach to social justice. Inclusion involves ensuring that all members of a community have a voice and are actively involved in decision-making processes. The text advocates for the empowerment of Black communities to confront and dismantle White supremacy. By addressing the dependent colonial status and the political and economic decisions made by colonial masters, the text challenges the exclusionary practices that have historically marginalized Black people. Inclusion requires dismantling these barriers and creating spaces where marginalized groups can thrive.

Conclusion

This chapter acts as a case study of the Black experience in a university setting, aiming to place a PWI in the broader scope of international and domestic relations as they shift and change over time. It showed how universities metabolized the Negro-Apocalypse through cultures of White supremacy that translate crisis into process and optics, and how the Scarborough Charter can either interrupt or reproduce that pattern depending on whether power (not just presence or representation) shifts. We named tactics (e.g. shadow strategies, racial conduits) that convert temporary fixes into durable change, and we located campus action within wider projects of reparative justice rather than representational DEI.

At times, we in the ivory towers of PWIs feel that we are immune to the outside global forces, which is funny to me because if we look at the first decade of existence of the institution where I am employed, global anti-colonial and decolonization movements were at the forefront of public consciousness and in university classrooms. The anti-Apartheid movements of the 1980s and 1990s were well-rooted in lecture halls and university quads. It is troubling to see the general capitalist shift of postsecondary education, particularly in Canada, since the 1990s that generally 'de-fanged' and 'de-politicized' the student body. This is why, I argue, the Negro-Apocalypse and its performative DEI salvo was so shocking to many; politics had returned to the consciousness of the youth. We now turn from principles and organizational logics to a campus-level archive: the University of Waterloo's 'Silent Years'. Chapter 6 asks how an institution born of Cold War pragmatism handled Black presence in the 1960s–70s, how immigration policy and national politics shaped that history, and what those patterns teach us about today's Charter-era commitments.

References

Alkalimat, A. (2021). *The history of Black studies.* Pluto Press.

Anderson, B. (1983). *Imagined communities: Reflections on the origin and spread of nationalism.* Verso Books.

Ansley, F. L. (1989). Stirring the ashes: Race, class and the future of civil rights scholarship. *Cornell Law Review, 74,* 993–1077. http://scholarship.law.cornell.edu/clr/vol74/iss6/1

Baldwin, J. (1993). *The fire next time.* Vintage Books.

Beckles, H. (2013). *Britain's Black debt: Reparations for Caribbean slavery and Native genocide.* University of West Indies Press.

Black Panther Party. (1967, May 15). What we want now! What we believe. *The Black Panther: Black Community News Service, 1*(2), 3. https://www.marxists.org/history/usa/pubs/black-panther/01n02-May%2015%201967.pdf

Blackett, A., Mukherjee Reed, A., Rigaud, M. C., Walker, B., Elisha, N., & Prashad, R. (2021). *Scarborough Charter on anti-Black racism and Black inclusion in Canadian higher education: Principles, actions, and accountabilities.* National Dialogues and Action for Inclusive Higher Education and Communities. https://www.utsc.utoronto.ca/scarborough-charter/

Caribbean Community (CARICOM). (2014). *Caricom ten point plan for reparatory justice.* https://caricom.org/caricom-ten-point-plan-for-reparatory-justice/

Caricom Reparations Commission (CRC). (2025). *10-point reparation plan.* CARICOM Reparations. https://caricomreparations.org/caricom/caricoms-10-point-reparation-plan/

Carrell, S. (2019, August 23). Glasgow University to pay £20m in slave trade reparations. *The Guardian.* https://www.theguardian.com/uk-news/2019/aug/23/glasgow-university-slave-trade-reparations

Fanon, F. (1963/2004). *The wretched of the earth* (R. Philcox, Trans.). Grove Press.

Farrah, D. (2020). Interrogating Malcolm X's "Ballot or the bullet". *Journal of African American Studies, 24,* 398–416. https://doi.org/10.1007/s12111-020-09484-5

Gosine, K. (2019). Moving on up' in the age of neo-liberalism: Reflections on Black middle-class consciousness and the implications for Black unity, leadership, and activism. In T. Kitossa, E. Lawson, & P. S. S. Howard (Eds.), *African Canadian leadership: Continuity, transition, and transformation* (pp. 241–262). University of Toronto Press.

Griffith, A. N., Hurd, N. M., & Hussain, S. B. (2017). "I didn't come to school for this": A qualitative examination of experiences with race-related stressors and coping responses among Black students attending a predominantly White institution. *Journal of Adolescent Research, 34*(2), 115–139. https://doi.org/10.1177/0743558417742983

Howard, P. S. S. (2019). Forging fortuity, asserting humanity: The emotional labour and resistance of Black racial equity leaders in predominantly White institutions. In T. Kitossa, E. S. Lawson, & P. S. S. Howard (Eds.), *African Canadian leadership: Continuity, transition, and transformation* (pp. 213–240). University of Toronto Press.

Kaba, M., & Hassan, S. (2019). *Fumbling towards repair: A workbook for community accountability facilitators.* Project NIA/Just Practice.

King, M. L., Jr. (1963, April 16). *Letter from a Birmingham jail [Letter, reproduced]*. African Studies Center, University of Pennsylvania. https://www.africa.upenn.edu/Articles_Gen/Letter_Birmingham.html

Lewis, S. F. (1997). Africana feminism: An alternative paradigm for Black women in the academy. In L. Benjamin (Ed.), *Black women in the academy: Promises and perils* (pp. 41–67). University Press of Florida.

Mathieson, G. (2002). Reconceptualizing our classroom practice: Notes from an anti-racist educator. In N. N. Wane, K. Deliovsky, & E. Lawson (Eds.), *Back to the drawing board: African Canadian feminisms* (pp. 158–174). Sumach Press.

Mensah, J., & Williams, C. J. (2017). *Boomerang ethics: How racism affects us all.* Fernwood Publishing.

Metzl, J. M. (2019). *Dying of whiteness: How the politics of racial resentment is killing America's heartland.* Basic Books.

Okun, T. (2017). *White supremacy culture.* Dismantling Racism Works. https://www.sbctc.edu/resources/documents/about/edi/White-supremacy-culture-tema-okun.pdf

Okun, T. (2021). *White supremacy culture – Still here.* White Supremacy Culture. http://www.whitesupremacyculture.info/

Patel, L. (2021). *No study without struggle: Confronting settler colonialism in higher education.* Beacon Press.

Taylor, C. S. (2020a, October 21-22). *The diachronic realities of confronting anti-Black racism* [Conference presentation]. Council on Inclusive Work Environments Canada. https://edata.conferenceboard.ca/docs/default-source/ciwe/oct2020_agenda_final.pdf?sfvrsn=e9e35f13_2

Taylor, C. S. (2020b). The racial conduit. In V. A. Young (Ed.), *This ain't yesterday's literacy: Culture and education after George Floyd.* Fountainhead Press.

Taylor, C. S. (2022). The Emigrant ambassadors: A foundation for present-day Black liberation. *Race & Class*, *63*(4), 107–117. https://doi.org/10.1177/03063968221083801

Thacker, R. S., & Freeman, S. (2021). "When I show up": Black provosts at predominantly white institutions. *Harvard Educational Review*, *91*(2), 157–178. https://doi.org/10.17763/1943-5045-91.2.157

Thompson, D. (2022). *The long road home: On Blackness and belonging.* Scribner Canada.

Ture, K. [Carmichael, S.], & Hamilton, C. V. (1967). *Black power: The politics of liberation in America.* Random House.

Walcott, R. (2021). *On property: Policing, prisons, and the call for abolition.* Biblioasis.

Wolfe, P. (2006). Settler colonialism and the elimination of the native. *Journal of Genocide Research*, *8*(4), 387–409. https://doi.org/10.1080/14623520601056240

Appendix A: Tema Okun's (2017, 2021) Notes on White Supremacy Culture

(1) *Perfectionism*: Little appreciation for others' work; recognition often goes to those already credited.

(2) *Sense of Urgency*: Rush to achieve results, hindering inclusivity and thoughtful decision-making; sacrifices interests of communities of colour for quick wins.
(3) *Defensiveness*: Structures protect existing power rather than fostering individual potential; energy spent defending against racism charges instead of addressing racism.
(4) *Quantity Over Quality*: Focus on measurable goals over quality relationships and democratic processes.
(5) *Worship of the Written Word*: Overemphasis on written documentation; undervaluing other forms of communication.
(6) *Only One Right Way*: Belief in a single correct approach; resistance to change seen as a fault in others.
(7) *Paternalism*: Decision-making power concentrated among a few; those in power make decisions for others.
(8) *Either/Or Thinking*: Binary thinking (good/bad, right/wrong); hinders learning from mistakes and accommodating conflict.
(9) *Power Hoarding*: Reluctance to share power; suggestions for change seen as threats.
(10) *Fear of Open Conflict*: Avoidance of conflict; discomfort with difficult issues leads to blaming the issue-raiser.
(11) *Individualism*: Preference for solo problem-solving; accountability directed upwards rather than sideways.
(12) *I'm the Only One*: Belief that one must do everything themselves; lack of delegation.
(13) *Progress is Bigger, More*: Success defined by expansion and serving more people, not necessarily better service.
(14) *Objectivity*: Belief in neutrality; invalidation of emotional responses.
(15) *Right to Comfort*: Equating individual unfairness against White people with systemic racism against people of colour.

Appendix B: Characteristics of a Racial Conduit and Anti-Racist Leader

The Key Behaviours of a Racial Conduit

- Understand and accept your positionality, and how others perceive you.
- Understand and accept the histories and realities of White supremacy, and how you benefit from it in the present.
- Understand how the systems you live and work within operate.
- Understand your individual, situational and institutional power.
- Sit in your truth: the truth of your White mediocrity, false sense of achievement and fabricated superiority.
- Use your (institutional, situation and institutional) power to create space for Black and racialized self-empowerment within systems.

- Give up your (institutional, situational and institutional) power once Black and racialized communities are embedded within systems.

Traits of an Anti-Racist Leader

- Has the courage to call out racism on institutional and individual levels, even if it may disadvantage their own personal or professional pursuits.
- 'Talks the talk' and 'walks the walk' (e.g. policies are created, and enforced at all times).
- Leads by example (i.e. uses anti-racist/oppressive language) and holds all staff accountable by ensuring the same is practised by the entire organization.
- Listens to, and acts on, any and all concerns faced by Black, Indigenous and racialized students and employees.
- Has the ability to take charge of systemic and interpersonal racism and take appropriate actions to investigate and address them.
- Understands who they are (self-awareness from an intersectional perspective), their position in the organization and how racialized and non-racialized people perceive them (e.g. a 360 that focuses on Privileges, Power, Position).
- Understands and acknowledges how systems and 'normal ways of being' marginalize, exclude and disadvantage racialized and Indigenous people.

Appendix C: Black Panther Party 10 Point Programme

(1) We want freedom. We want power to determine the destiny of our Black community.
(2) We want full employment for our people.
(3) We want an end to the robbery by the White man of our Black community.
(4) We want decent housing, fit for the shelter of human beings.
(5) We want education for our people that exposes the true nature of this decadent American society.
(6) We want education that teaches us our true history and our role in the present-day society. We want all Black men to be exempt from military service.
(7) We want an immediate end to police brutality and murder (author's emphasis) of Black people.
(8) We want freedom for all Black men held in federal, state, county and city prisons and jails.
(9) We want all Black people when brought to trial to be tried in court by a jury of their peer group or people from their Black communities. As defined by the Constitution of the United States.
(10) We want land, bread, housing, education, clothing, justice and peace (Black Panther Party, 1967, p. 3).

Chapter 6

The Silent Years: Black Presence at the University of Waterloo, 1960s–1970s

Why This Case, and Why Now?

Having mapped how universities manage crises in Chapter 5, this chapter turns to a concrete archive: the University of Waterloo (UW). We ask how an institution engineered for Cold War industry and co-op innovation recorded (or refused to record) Black presence, and how that archival silence became a technology of belonging, in other words, the foundation of DEI in an institution. The goal is not collecting and presenting a piece of the past; it is to surface the long prehistory of today's Scarborough Charter-era promises and the organizational habits that make them fragile.

UW's founding coalition framed higher education as a national solution to a manpower crisis, an orientation to production and partnership that shaped what counted as value and who counted as a fit. When Black presence appears in the record, it is often as sojourner or exception, for example, international students framed as development targets, or 'firsts' whose recognition doubles as institutional self-absolution. These patterns are not anomalies; they are consistent with the appeasement DEI logics analysed in Chapter 5 and throughout this book.

As Black student and faculty presence ticked up in the 1960s, wider politics – immigration regimes, 'Canadianization', and the fallout from the Sir George Williams Affair – helped re-secure boundaries. The result was a prolonged period in which Black faculty hiring stagnated and Black experience was rendered exterior to the university's story. These are the Silent Years, silent not due to absence, but due to managed invisibility. By reading catalogues, newspapers, interviews and policy debates together, we show how archival silence operates as an instrument of institutional Whiteness and how that history clarifies the limits of contemporary reforms premised on representation without redistribution. I would like to

Unmasking DEI, 89–104

doi:10.1108/978-1-83708-356-520261006

acknowledge the work of Jonathan Zi En Chan for his research assistantship in developing sections of this chapter.

The Tales of a Second-Generation Bajan Navigating Higher Learning

Growing up in the Greater Toronto Area (GTA) in Canada in a Bajan household, I was very comfortable existing in non-White spaces. Yes, I knew how to survive – and thrive – in predominantly White spaces, but for me, being among my primordial kin was always something that was, and is, very important to me. As I've gotten older, I've expanded this understanding of 'primordial' and 'kin', but family, and roots and routes, are always my priorities. So, it makes sense that I did not do, even if I had the opportunities, what many academics do in pursuit of an 'academic job; ' I did not follow the job market anywhere in the world. For the research I do in Black Studies, I could have gone to the United States, but I was reluctant to do that, even during an Obama administration. I had possibilities of venturing to the African Continent, but never pursued those with any real conviction. Home is important to me. Home is life. Home is my safety net.

However, I defended my dissertation at a time where there were even fewer jobs for 'Black stuff' in the humanities, social sciences, and liberal arts compared to now. DEI wasn't a thing, and CRT and Black Studies had yet to reach the fever point of mainstream academic recognition. So, I did what any other parent-fearing, second-generation child did; I went out and got a job. That being said, academia was always the goal, so when I saw a job ad in 2017 for a contract teaching position at the UW, I took it and started in a teaching role in 2018.

Why the UW? Choosing the Anti-Black Landscape

The choice for Waterloo, like many PhD graduates looking for work, was an opportunity to get back into a classroom. The big added bonus was that it was on the 401 corridor (about an hour drive west from the GTA on the Trans-Canada highway in Ontario). I didn't have to uproot my life or leave my family, like many academics have to do while on the job market. In fact, my drive to Waterloo was shorter than my daily commute while working in my previous career in government. I also knew the drive quite well. I did my masters and PhD in London, Ontario (about an hour drive west of Waterloo region). I did research on Black communities throughout southern and southwestern Ontario and knew quite well what I was getting myself into by going back into the area. This part of Ontario does have a rich history of Black history, particularly as it relates to Free Black communities that settled following the US' *Fugitive Slave Act* of 1850 and as terminus of the Underground Railroad. However, the region also has a rich history of anti-Black racism, the KKK, and historical evidence (even gathered by UW historians) of the settlement of Nazis following the

Second World War. In 2023, Waterloo region had the highest rate of police-reported hate crimes in Canada. Of those that were reported as hate against one's ethnicity, half were against Black people (Brown, 2024).

So yes, I willingly chose to live in one of the most anti-Black cities in Canada to do DEI and other 'Black' work. That all being said, it is key to understand that most people know very little of these (positive and negative) histories. I will openly say that my engagement at UW was not an act of martyrdom, but an intentional one; my eyes were wide open to the deliberate historical and contemporary silencing of Black voices in this region.

The UW is a reflection of the region it was born into. There is an obvious exclusion of Black participation from the recorded history of the school. Despite the institution coming into existence during a time of global student activism and politicization, there was very little evidence of 'DEI' or social justice initiatives or political leanings. Digging through the archives since 1957, I could see that for every year that passed, Blackness was virtually experienced outside of the university, not within. Yes, there were Black 'firsts' – the first Black professor, the first Black student cohort – a reflection of the multicultural tenets of appeasement DEI. This is a core example of the machinations of a DEI in a Predominantly White Institution (PWI): Blackness is contained and tokenized or it happens over '*there*' but not '*here*'. This is very reminiscent of appeasement DEI's 'colourblind' approach.

Anti-Blackness at the UW

The literature representing staff, admin and students alike reported Blackness as an experience outside of the institution. It didn't belong in the ivory towers. Blackness was music to enjoy in town. Blackness was to be consumed in movie theatres. Blackness was acceptable if it served the White moral campus along the lines of interest convergence or created a morally righteous standpoint. Blackness was bundled under foreign and international students. Blackness was the occasional freedom of speech debate topic. And yet, Blackness was not Waterloo. Whether academics and administrators in PWIs across the globe want to admit it or not, the 'outside world' impacts the day-to-day operations of these institutions. Since 1957, there have been key dates in world affairs that *should* have been key definers, or at least archival speaking points, on the UW campus.

This school has always had Black people in it. However, from the sources that we look at in the archives pre-Negro-Apocalypse, it would seem like they were rare, oftentimes only there in a 'look at the favour we did for you' type of way. Blackness was described at the school as foreign. Blackness is foreign for the school. The Black 'outsider' was highlighted as the *benevolent* foreign student. It is clear that the founders and gatekeepers of UW wanted to keep Blackness out, and did so by refusing to give Black people the space to begin with. The absence of them in the historical record, particularly in something as free and expressive as a student newspaper, highlighted the gatekeeping of belonging. A gatekeeping that made the Negro-Apocalypse of 2020 a catastrophic shock to the White supremacist institution's system.

A History of the UW

On 4 April 1956, Gerald Hagey, Ira Needles, along with the first board of governors, incorporated Waterloo College Associate Faculties (WCAF), which then became the present-day UW. Hagey and Needles had a dream; they realized the Canadian economy was in desperate need of engineers, scientists and other technical professionals, and hoped to establish a new university based on the co-operative education plan to serve those needs (Redmond, 2016b). They believed that by partnering with industries across Canada, WCAF would be able to train students to become technological professionals that were immediately employable by companies upon graduation. The approach Hagey and Needles took to realize their vision and to create a university based on this unique curriculum was unique and innovative, and the spirit of innovation continues to rest upon UW today. However, despite the glowing recollections of the strides the founders took to establish the university, UW was not immune to social perceptions in Canadian society at the time. The objective of the present chapter is to re-examine the history of UW in its first two decades within the context of the Cold War and the changing discourse on immigration by Peoples of Colour in the 1970s, offering possible explanations as to why Black faculty at UW was on the decline starting in the late 1960s.

A College for the Cold War

In 1955, Waterloo College reached out to Gerald Hagey, then the national public relations and advertising manager of B. F. Goodrich, to become the next president of the College (Redmond, 2016a). Before taking up this new position, Hagey reached out to Ira Needles, the president of B. F. Goodrich Canada, for advice since both men had the heart to contribute to the betterment of society. Needles understood the attraction Hagey had towards the offer and became a staunch collaborator in this new endeavour (Scott, 1967). The position Hagey was considering had many pressing issues, with the predominant concern centring on the continual development of the college itself. He was well-aware that even the growing Lutheran congregation was unable to keep up with the expenses of the Waterloo College (Redmond, 2016a). Hagey considered applying for government funding, but that door was closed to him; the Ontario government, under the premiership of Leslie Frost, would not contribute taxpayer dollars to any denominational colleges and universities. However, there was a way around this obstacle. By setting up a non-denominational faculty, University of Ottawa and University of Windsor managed to receive funds despite being affiliated with a denominational university (Strömbergsson-Denora, 2020). Gerald Hagey conceived the plan to follow this path and sought to establish

WCAF, which would serve as the non-denominational faculty of science for Waterloo College (Redmond, 2016a).

WCAF was, in part, established to contribute to Canadian aims during the Cold War. Canada was not keeping pace with the technological developments in the Soviet Union and this became a matter of national concern (Redmond, 2016b). The foremost issue was the desperate need for technological professionals, engineers and technicians, and how to fulfil that need. Shortly after the incorporation of WCAF, Ira Needles gave a speech to the Rotary Club titled 'Wanted: 150,000 Engineers and Technicians – The Waterloo Plan' (McLaughlin, 1997, p. 39) and presented a solution of how the Associate Faculties could contribute to addressing the economic needs of Canadian society as well as its Cold War aims. The 'Waterloo Plan' proposed a close partnership between educators and industrialists by having students train under various participating companies in a co-operative education scheme that would rotate four months of school with four months of work (Redmond, 2016b). Needles believed that the co-operative education would provide industries with students that would become 'familiar with industry operations' when they graduate. Two months after Needles' speech, in September of 1956, the leading industrialists convened a National Conference on Engineering, Scientific and Technical Manpower at St. Andrews-by-the-Sea in New Brunswick (McLaughlin, 1997). The objective of the conference was to discuss the pace of technological developments in Canada relative to the Soviet Union and the expansion of higher education to meet those needs. Needles circulated a copy of the 'Waterloo Plan' in advance to the industrialists attending the conference and the Plan was met with optimism and support. Kenneth McLaughlin (1997) states that even though many of the attendees at the conference may not have heard of the newly established Associate Faculties, they certainly were aware of Ira Needles and his accomplishments in industry and lent their support to the plan.

The Waterloo Plan: Innovation Defines the University

The Waterloo Plan was a very ambitious, innovative plan that many other university administrators held with scepticism. The co-operative education system was not the traditional means of training engineers, and many felt the quality of engineers graduating from Associate Faculties would suffer as a result (McLaughlin, 1997). However, desperate times called for desperate measures. The speech that Ira Needles gave at the Rotary Club that was later sensationally named 'Wanted 150,000' by the Globe and Mail highlights the uneasy atmosphere in Canadian politics with regards to achieving Cold War aims and expanding higher education (McLaughlin, 1997).

> In addition, there are [1.5] million students at 4,000 technical schools in Russia; as these young people graduate, they will feed and sustain the Soviet professional manpower pool. It is very evident that Russian leaders are creating new generations of educated, young people who are learning to think clearly and

> deeply. As education in the scientific fields is introduced to Russians, their thought processes are bound to develop beyond the merely scientific. Sooner or later, they will take a penetrating look at our democratic, free enterprise way of life. (Needles, 1956, p. 3)

The quotation reiterates the potential consequences if Canada was unable to keep up with the colossal Russian education system in producing engineers and is accompanied by a warning to Canadians in Cold War rhetoric. However, to say WCAF was founded simply to produce engineers in the technological race within the Cold War would be misleading. The founders, Hagey and Needles, while business leaders concerned and involved in national affairs, were still philanthropists at heart. They were aware of the costs of higher education and the pitfalls of failing out of a technical programme, seeking to safeguard the students they intended to recruit from both. By providing a six-year programme starting with non-technical subjects, the founders hoped that students would have an easier transition from high school and become 'well-rounded' individuals in society, similar to the graduates the Russians were training en masse in the quotation (Needles, 1956). At the same time, the co-operative plan also reduced the financial burden of higher education by allowing students to earn a small income at various companies while gaining practical experience (Needles, 1956). I assert that though Hagey and Needles were people of the Cold War era and preoccupied with Canadian Cold War objectives, they were still invested in the futures of the next generation. At the same time, their altruism cannot be divorced from the ideologies of the time.

Black Presence in the 1960s

Black Power and decolonization movements were concurrent with the developments of the Cold War. Black peoples around the world saw education as the pathway to social mobility and an effective policy to enrich their societies. As a result, many universities in Britain, United States, Canada, and the Union of Soviet Socialist Republics (USSR) were hosts to 'sojourning' Black students from Africa and the Caribbean (Chan, 2021; Concordia University, 2023; McCartney, 2016). However, these travelling Black students were seen as a threat to Canadian society by the end of the decade.

Without ethnic data of students that were enrolled at the UW, it would be difficult to pinpoint who, when and from where the first Black students arrived on campus. The earliest notable documentation of students includes a photo of Douglas Wright, Dean of Engineering, with students that came to UW through an initiative later known as the 'Kennedy Airlift'.[1] In 1959, a Kenyan named Tom Mboya began an initiative, with the collaboration with African Student Foundation, to send students from East Africa to North American universities. The initiative received the name 'Kennedy Airlift' because of a timely donation by Senator John F. Kennedy to pay for the airfare of the students just as the funds for the operation were depleting. UW also welcomed several students from Nigeria, all of them won scholarships from the African Student Foundation, the organizer of the airlift.[2] One of those students Frederick Layode was interviewed by *The Coryphaeus*, a UW student newspaper. Frederick, also known as Jimmy, was asked about other African students of the airlift and his future plans. He replied that many students enrolled in science programmes and he planned to eventually 'go back to one's country and help' (Sanders, 1962, p. 2).

Not All Altruistic Motives: The Interest Convergence of Opening the Door to Black International Students

Similar to the altruistic goals that the founders of UW had in trying to reduce the financial burden of their prospective students, accepting international students into North American universities was not without an ulterior motive. Dale McCartney (2016) argues that from the end of the Second World War to 1969, Canadian parliamentarians saw international students as 'development targets', and they were not allowed to stay in Canada upon graduation (p. 4). The students deemed 'worthy' were provided with the means to complete their post-secondary education in Canada. Afterwards, these students would return to their home countries with their newly acquired skills and contribute to the development of their home countries, which the Canadian government constitutes as a form of foreign aid. They were also instilled with ideas of democracy in hopes they return to their home country with a sense of goodwill and even act as ambassadors of democracy (McCartney, 2016). Therefore, the students were both the targets for development while in Canada receiving their education and the agents of development when they returned home. Despite the apparent 'generosity' of the Canadian government, the students were often treated with high-handed paternalism upon arrival. In 1960, there was a case where a West Indian student studying in Ottawa lost a part of his funding because he visited some of his relatives in another province upon their invite. International students had to inform Ottawa before travelling to another province or risk losing their monthly allowance. In this particular case, the West Indian student was denied his monthly allowance and had to pay back half of the funding from the month before (Bush, 1960).

Black Communities Finding 'Diversity' and 'Inclusion' in the 1960s at the UW

The 1960s was an exciting time at the UW. It was a period of rapid expansion where the founders pushed the boundaries against the traditions of higher education with their innovative spirit. Professors from various disciplines joined UW because they knew they had the freedom to experiment with new pedagogical methods. During this period, African and Caribbean students studying at UW were a small minority that had difficulty fitting in (*The Coryphaeus*, 1968). It was not until the 1970s when the Black student body grew in numbers that student groups, like the African Student Association and the Caribbean Student

Association, began organizing various events such as talks on decolonization, cultural exchange and social gatherings. On the other hand, there was much greater activity in Black faculty.

To keep pace with the growing enrolment and expansion of the university, administrators appointed many new professors and hired many lecturers with some pathways to advancement. The Black faculty members at UW in the 1960s had a large impact not only on the local community, but also on the international community as well. Locksley Edmondson was the first Black professor at UW (Glaser, 2017). Although he stayed with the university for a few short years in the Political Science department, he was later the chair of multiple United Nations Educational, Scientific and Cultural Organization (UNESCO) meetings on Caribbean culture and migration. Another professor in the same department, Cedric Grant, also taught for a few years at UW before pursuing diplomatic work full time (Osanku, 2007). He served as the High Commissioner to the United Kingdom and the Ambassador to the United States in Guyana. Leonard Fletcher from the Economics department was a founding member of the Kitchener-Waterloo Caribbean Canadian Cultural Association (now known as the Caribbean Canadian Association of Waterloo Region, CCAWR), a group that continues to serve members and students of the community in the present day (Waterloo Region Record, 2021). In the same department, Karl Bennett, who was hired slightly later than Fletcher, served as a professor until his retirement in 2002 (CCAWR, n.d.). During his tenure, he was on many prominent committees such as the Ontario Premier's Council on Economic Renewal and United Nations (UN) Caribbean Regional Integration Advisory Team. To this day, Dr Bennett continues to be an active member of the Caribbean Canadian Association of Waterloo Region. And from Sociology, Donald M'Timkulu was a popular professor and remembered for his courses on Race and Culture (Renison University College, 2023). He established the beginning of the Applied Social Science programme and was heavily involved with UW's Canadian University Service Overseas (CUSO) committee. These are just some examples of the impact that Black faculty hired in the 1960s had on Waterloo and other communities abroad. Whether these professors stayed with UW or left to pursue other interests, they had an immense heart for bettering communities in Canada and their countries of origin. However, the nature of Black presence in the faculties of UW changed with the sentiments on immigration by peoples of colour throughout the 1960s.

Changing Perceptions

Patterns Repeat Themselves: The B(l)acklash of 'Liberal' Immigration Policies in Canada

The issue of immigration has always been a heated subject in White Canadian society. Despite ratifying the Universal Declaration of Human Rights in 1948, where signatory countries were to hold all as 'equal before the law and are entitled without any discrimination to equal protection of the law' (Article 7),

Canadian immigration policy was still rife with racial discrimination. The 'colour line' to immigration was finally removed in 1962 when Minister of Citizenship and Immigration Ellen Fairclough amended the *Immigration Act* to eliminate overt racial discrimination and prioritized skill as the main criteria for applicants looking to settle in the country. It was a small step forward to de-racializing immigration, but many commentators and activists still questioned whether the new skill criterion was merely the colour line in a different form. In an editorial to the *Globe and Mail*, an anonymous person wrote:

> Canada has no formal color bar against West Indians of African descent. Yet, by acting on the assumption that no West Indian could possibly earn a living in Canada, the Department has kept the immigration from the islands to a mere trickle. (Anonymous, 1962, p. 6)

Indeed, immigration from the Caribbean ranged from 3% of the total immigration to Canada to slowly grew to 6.8% in 1968. In comparison, immigration from Western Europe, with British immigrants being the largest group of them all, totalled over 80% of the annual immigration into Canada within the same period (Statistics Canada, 2015). The statistics revealed that despite the fact skill was the primary criteria for admission into Canada, the enforcement of the immigration policies still resulted in predominantly White immigration.

The island nations of the Caribbean had a closer tie to Canada, as they shared membership within the British Commonwealth and had established trade relationships. In terms of trade, Canada and the West Indies were mostly symbiotic; Canada needed West Indian agricultural staples and the West Indies needed Canadian manufactured goods and a large export market (Taylor, 2016). However, as I have argued elsewhere, Canada possessed greater economic power and was able to force Barbados and the rest of the West Indies, to accept the ideological terms of their relationship, which included the immigration issue (Taylor, 2016). Nations in the West Indies wanted the Canadian government to relax the immigration policy to take up more unskilled workers. However, the contrary was happening. The skill requirement in the post-1962 Canadian immigration policy led to a greater brain drain of skilled workers from the West Indies, workers that were desperately needed in the Caribbean to help development at home. In an article, G. Arthur Brown, the Director of the Jamaican Government's central planning unit, was cited:

> We have a shortage of these people [skilled workers], just as you have in Canada, and we don't want them to go. But you can offer them more attractive salaries, perhaps a better life, and they are leaving. It is beginning to constitute a serious problem. (Green, 1962, p. 7)

But it was evident that Canada did not want unskilled labour from anywhere, perhaps except from countries that were predominantly White. Black unskilled immigration was often seen as the root cause of epidemics of crime in whichever city they settled in. Throughout the 1960s, there were many letters to newspapers that voiced their fears of Black immigration will create 'Black ghettos' and 'Toronto Harlem' (Anonymous, 1969a, p. 6; Sawyer, 1966, p. 6). Thus, the common justification of the time to reject unskilled Black immigrants was always to cite insufficient capacity within the Canadian economy to absorb them and provide them with jobs that would keep them out of trouble.

Disaggregating the 'Skilled' From the 'Unskilled'

After briefly discussing the discourse on Black unskilled labour, how did Canadian society view Black skilled labour? Canada needed skilled workers to contribute to its continued economic expansion and achieve its Cold War aims. Carl Pollock, one of the founders of UW and president of Dominion Electrohome Industries Ltd., commented in a mid-1960s talk that Canada needed at least 200,000 immigrants per year to 'speed up the growth' of population and manufacturing activity (Anonymous, 1963, p. 6). Canadians were aware of their need for immigration to stimulate the economy, especially skilled labour; but year after year, they also wondered why there were so few people of colour immigrating into Canada.

Two interviews with Immigration Minister John Nicholson provide some insight into that question. In an interview conducted in 1965, Nicholson gave contradictory comments regarding Caribbean immigration. He first said, 'Our rapid expansion is creating jobs in skilled and professional categories faster than we can produce qualified workers through Canadian sources', and then cites statistics that the schools can only meet 2% of the job vacancies (Anonymous, 1965a, p. 27). Then, he states that more immigration offices would be opened in England, Italy, and possibly in Japan and the Philippines. However, when asked about his position on immigration from the West Indies, he said, 'West Indians are welcomed to come to Canada, but they are needed in the Caribbean countries which have a far greater need for technical and professional people' (Anonymous, 1965a, p. 27). A month later in another interview. when asked whether there is a colour bar in Canadian immigration policy, Nicholson replied:

> The answer is that most of the people who apply for immigration to Canada from parts of the world where you refer to the residents as colored do not have the professional and other skills that render them admissible to Canada without sponsorship. (Anonymous, 1965b, p. 7)

There was a desperate need for skilled workers in 1960s Canada that could not be fulfilled by the Canadian education system; thus, policymakers looked to immigration of skilled labour. However, the two interviews with Nicholson highlight the type of immigration Canada wanted, namely White and Asian *only if necessary*, with undesired immigration being blocked with various justifications. I echo an argument I have previously published, that Canadian immigration was purposely kept arbitrary to evade charges of racism. And, with regards to labour, Blacks and racialized peoples were kept away with justifications that incited Canadian fears of lowering wages and employment competition with White Canadian workers (Taylor, 2016).

In retrospect, the discourse against the employment of racialized peoples to fill certain capacities within the Canadian economy has not changed in the past century. In the 1880s, there was a similar debate on whether Chinese labourers should be employed to build the Canadian Pacific Railway. John A. Macdonald said to the Parliament in 1882, 'It is simply a question of alternatives, either you must have this labour, or you can't have the railway' (Oliver, 2021, p. 36). Employing racialized workers in Canada was always a last resort and a lesser of two evils. The arguments against Chinese immigration in the late 19th century bear striking similarities to the resistance to Black immigration in the 1970s, that the Chinese would lower wages and steal jobs from White Canadians, that they brought vices that would corrupt the social fabric, or that they were simply sojourners not planning to stay. The final justification against Chinese immigration was reapplied to international students; the Canadian government made sure that the students knew they were not welcome to stay before embarking on their education in Canada. As immigration from the West Indies increased in the late 1960s, so did the temperature of racial tensions in Canadian society, which finally erupted in events of social unrest in parts of Canada.

The Sir George Williams Affair

29 January 1969. Four hundred students occupied a computer lab at Sir George Williams University because the university administrators brushed aside an accusation against Perry Anderson, a biology professor, for purposely giving Black students in his class lower grades. A peaceful settlement was initially achieved on February 10th, but when the students realized that the university had no intention of taking their concerns seriously, they elevated the occupation. The police were called in to storm the occupied building and a fire mysteriously broke out. Some students threw computer punch cards out of the windows during the altercation. In the aftermath, aside from arrests made by the police against student protests, both Black and White, the incident became known in the Caribbean. Roland Michener, the Governor General of Canada, who was in Trinidad and Tobago as part of a tour of the Caribbean, was unable to present a speech at University of the West Indies because of the vigorous protests of the students on campus who stood in solidarity with those in Sir George Williams University.

Sean Mills (2010) argues that the Sir George Williams Affair, as this incident came to be known, grew out of tensions caused by racial injustice in Montreal and across the globe, and that 'local events acquired their meaning when they were read through larger narratives of anti-colonialism' (p. 107). In a sense, if such an incident did not manifest itself at Sir George William University, it would have elsewhere. Statistics show that the proportion of immigration that came from the West Indies increased from 2.78% in 1966 to 5–6% in 1967 and 1968, and 15% in 1969 (Statistics Canada, 2015). Canadians were simply apprehensive at the number of Black immigrants entering 'their' country and perhaps the rising of the Black power movements globally. In the aftermath of the incident, parliamentarians and the Canadian public were quick to call for the deportation of the 'menacing' students. In response to Immigration Minister Allan MacEachen's vow to check the immigration status of the arrested student protesters, an editorial pointed out that many people who had nothing to do with the riot would be stereotyped because of their country of origin (Anonymous, 1969b).

Closing the Door Once Black People Challenge the Racist System

As racial tensions elevated in the late 1960s, there was a change in sentiment on what the international student meant to the Canadian public. In 1967, parliamentarians began questioning whether the expenses spent on international students were justified. MP Raymond Langlois argued that student aid was a waste if the students were not returning to their home country but settling in Canada instead, which defeated the purpose of having the students act as the target of foreign aid (McCartney, 2016). McCartney (2016) claims that the changing discourse from seeing international students as worthy of aid to them being dangerous potential immigrants was not a coincidence. The justification to end 'foreign aid' via international students was framed by two means: that the students were unqualified landed immigrants and could potentially be political radicals, and they posed as economic competition against Canadian students (McCartney, 2016). The Canadian government reduced the number of students by the summer of 1969 and the effects were immediately felt. During interviews with retired professors at UW, many of them commented on the marked decline of students from the Caribbean (personal communication, 12 August 2021). If there was a stark drop in the number of international students following the Sir George Williams Affair, how did Black faculty fare?

The Silent Years

More than one department at UW did not hire a single Black faculty member from the 1970s to the 2000s (Anonymous professor, personal communication, 13 February 2022). Was this phenomenon simply an extension of Sir George Williams Affair or was there more to uncover? While there is no definite answer to this question, I endeavour to offer some possible explanations on how prevailing social trends in the 1970s could have affected Black presence at UW. Parallel to the Black movements that indirectly shaped the discourse on Black immigration in Canada, there was also the Canadianization movement, where the public feared the influence of foreigners in higher education upon the next generation of (White) Canadians.

The Great White North: The Canadianization Movement

The Canadianization movement began around 1968, one year after MP Langlois raised concerns about the continual 'investment' of Canadian taxpayer dollars into international students, which led to a government commission. The Commission on Canadian Studies chaired by T. H. B. Symons, the former President of Trent University, called for universities to be fairer to Canadian applicants and to increase the level of Canadian content in courses. Silva et al. (1988) argue that the commission was a 'symbolic crusade', where 'nationalists seeing an expanding higher learning increasingly staffed by non-Canadians felt their social honour threatened' (p. 140). Furthermore, they claim the commission report mostly supported the administration of university managers (Silva et al., 1988). The statistics on the percentage of professors who were persons of colour reveal an interesting revelation. The data from a study by Max von Zur-Muehlen (1983) shows that the proportion of newly appointed full-time university teachers labelled as originating from 'other Commonwealth' and 'other countries', which I used as a proxy for applicants that could be considered coming from a non-White country, totalled between 6-7% of all appointments from 1972 to 1983 (p. 34). The proportion of Canadian teachers increased from 59.1% in 1972 to 76.4% in 1983 mostly at the expense of a declining number of American and British professors. Within the period of the study, approximately 960–1400 new teachers were appointed per year (Von Zur-Muehlen, 1983). This meant that the proportion of university teachers who were non-White was not affected by the Canadianization movement.

For departments at UW to be unable to hire a single qualified Black professor in 30 years is too much of a 'coincidence' given that there was no marked decline in applicants from countries that were predominantly non-White. Perhaps, the innovative spirit of UW did not render itself immune to prevailing social discourses. Recalling the vigorous activity by certain Black professors in the 1960s, the lack of Black presence in the faculties of UW meant, to a certain extent, innovation and community building by Black professors were stifled during 'the Silent Years'.

Lessons for the Scarborough Charter Era: Without Power Shift, History Repeats as Policy Theatre

The UW found success by addressing the problems of Canadian society during the Cold War. During the Negro-Apocalypse, other PWIs across the Black Atlantic have committed to understanding their legacies of enslavement and anti-Black racism. With this case study of the UW as it relates to present-day appeasement to DEI and anti-Blackness policies, it is critically important for researches to go beyond the explicit cases of racism. Just because a founder of a PWI did not own enslaved people, or was not an architect of Residential Schools, does not mean that the function of the institution itself was not constructed as products of oppression and anti-Blackness. We must not forget that the function of capitalism is predicated on the existence of racism. We must not forget that the Cold War was a battle of 'Capitalism' vs 'Communism'. We cannot divorce the founding of the University in the 1950s from the post-War de-colonialization movements across the African Continent and the Black Atlantic, and how those movements were rooted in East vs West ideological supports. In order for us to understand how it responded to the Negro-Apocalypse, we must understand its original purpose to exist.

The founders Gerald Hagey and Ira Needles were concerned with Cold War aims and the necessity to expand the capacity for technological development in the Canadian economy. This was done by training legions of skilled engineers and scientists to meet the Cold War-centred need of the industries to keep pace with Russian technological investments while also reducing the burden of their students in pursuing what would have been an expensive education. The philanthropic altruism of the founders could not be divorced from their ideologies. In the end, despite the innovative approach of UW to experiment with pedagogy in higher education, it too was not immune to prevailing social discourse. This was evident in the lack of presence of Black faculty starting in the 1970s. In the present day, many of the issues that Canadian society faces require different expertise and are problems with deep, complex historical and social implications: decolonization, anti-racism and upholding equity and human rights. There is no doubt that UW can maintain itself as one of the top technical institutions of North America, but will it rise again to the challenges of today and boldly contribute to solving the issues in society as the founders, Gerald Hagey and Ira Needles, once did during its establishment? Can it do this in an environment where appeasement DEI continues to hide the truth?

Conclusion

This chapter reassembled disparate artefacts (speeches, student journalism, personnel patterns, immigration debates, among others) into a story of managed (in)visibility: Black students and faculty were present, impactful and networked, yet were routinely rendered adjacent to the university's self-image. Naming this chapter as The Silent Years clarifies how today's appeasement DEI scripts can re-create the same dynamic under new labels. The implication for current reformers is stark; archives, governance and budgets must change together or representation collapses back into appeasement.

The next chapter turns from archival diagnosis to design questions: What would it take – structurally and ideologically – to ensure that Black Flourishing and Accountability are not slogans but consequential commitments? What would it look like if we had historical, contemporary and futurist Black-first ways of being as our signposts for foundational and radical change? We will outline decision-right shifts, reparative funding models and governance reforms that operationalize the lessons of Chapters 5 and 6 in policy and practice.

Notes

1. The Nigerian engineering students identified in the photo with Douglas Wright were Adesanya Akadri, Oluremi Balogum, and Samuel Ilechukwu.
2. Five scholarship winners were David Umeh from East Nigeria, Olapade Fadane, Olatokunboh Oshinowo, Oduola Layoye, and Frederick Layode from Western Nigeria.

References

Anonymous. (1962, January 22). *The opening door*. Globe and Mail.

Anonymous. (1963, November 25). *Poor performance*. Globe and Mail.

Anonymous. (1965, July 10). *Skills needed: Plans would search to fill 150,000 jobs*. Globe and Mail.

Anonymous. (1965, August 20). *Canada: In search of a population*. Globe and Mail.

Anonymous. (1969, February 15). *Not necessarily inevitable*. Globe and Mail.

Anonymous. (1969, April 14). *The unsupported suspicion of Canadian racism*. Globe and Mail.

Brown, D. (2024, October 5). Waterloo region has the highest rate of police-reported hate crimes in Canada. What police, advocates are saying. *CBC News*. https://www.cbc.ca/news/canada/kitchener-waterloo/waterloo-region-police-reported-hate-crimes-1.7341666

Bush, R. S. (1960, December 9). *Traveling students*. Globe and Mail.

Chan, J. Z. E. (2021, October 18). *A brief history of Black experience at Waterloo, 1960s-1990s*. University of Waterloo. https://uwaterloo.ca/news/arts/brief-history-black-experience-waterloo-1960s-1990s

Concordia University. (2023, May 18). *1969 Sir Geoge Williams University student protest: Historical context*. https://www.concordia.ca/about/history/1969-student-protest/historical-context.html#bibliography

Glaser, L. B. (2017, April 6). *Africana symposium to honor Locksley Edmondson*. Cornell Chronicle. https://news.cornell.edu/stories/2017/04/africana-symposium-honor-locksley-edmondson

Green, R. (1962). *A gesture turned sour for Jamaica*. Globe and Mail.

McCartney, D. M. (2016). Inventing international students: Exploring discourses in international student policy talk, 1945-75. *Historical Studies in Education*, *28*(2). https://doi.org/10.32316/hse/rhe.v28i2.4457

McLaughlin, K. (1997). *Waterloo: The unconventional founding of an unconventional university*. University of Waterloo.

Mills, S. (2010). *The empire within: Postcolonial thought and political activism in sixties Montreal*. McGill-Queen's University Press.

Needles, I. G. (1956, August 27). *Wanted: 150,000 engineers and technicians—The Waterloo Plan*. University of Waterloo Archives Collection. https://digital.library.uwaterloo.ca/uwdl-79b98afa-269a-46b7-82d9-04632abd5d4b/wanted-150000-engineers-and-technicians-waterloo-plan#page/1/mode/1up

Oliver, D. C. (2021). *Beyond the railway narrative: Exclusion and agency in Chinese Canadian history before 1947* (Master's thesis, Saint Mary's University). Patrick Power Library Repository. https://library2.smu.ca/handle/01/30611

Osanku, M. (2007). *Obituary: Dr. Cedric Hilburn Grant (April 23, 1936–June 15, 2005)*. Guyana Genealogical and Biographical Society. https://guygenbiosociety.blogspot.com/2007/12/dr-cedric-hilburn-grant-1935-june-15.html

Redmond, C. (2016a, October 10). *How it all began*. University of Waterloo. https://uwaterloo.ca/innovation60/blog/post/how-it-all-began

Redmond, C. (2016b, October 17). *Wanted: 150,000 engineers*. University of Waterloo. https://uwaterloo.ca/innovation60/blog/post/wanted-150000-engineers

Renison University College. (2023, February 27). *Celebrating the contributions of Dr M'Timkulu*. University of Waterloo. https://uwaterloo.ca/renison/news/celebrating-contributions-dr-mtimkulu

Sanders, S. (1962, October 5). Profile. *The Coryphaeus*, *3*(2), 2. http://s3.amazonaws.com/UWPublications/Imprint/1962-63_v3/1962-63_v3,n02_Coryphaeus.pdf

Sawyer, D. B. (1966, January 20). *Letters to the editor: Immigration*. Globe and Mail.

Scott, J. (1967). *Of mud and dreams: University of Waterloo 1957–1967*. Ryerson Press.

Silva, E., Pupo, N., & Green, B. (1988). Foreign scholars, Canadian content: Symbolic politics and the Symons Report. *McGill Journal of Education*, *23*(2). https://mje.mcgill.ca/article/view/7810

Statistics Canada. (2015, November 5). *Table no 43-10-0002-01: Historical statistics, immigration to Canada, by country of last permanent residence, 1956 to 1976 [Data tables]*. https://doi.org/10.25318/4310000201-eng

Strömbergsson-Denora, A. (2020). *Warring sovereignties: Church control and state pressure at the University of Ottawa*. University of Ottawa Press.

Taylor, C. S. (2016). *Flying fish in the great white north: The autonomous migration of Black Barbadians*. Fernwood Publishing.

The Caribbean Canadian Association of Waterloo Region (CCAWR). (n.d.). *Meet our committee*. [Dr. Karl Bennett]. https://www.ccawr.ca/ccawr-scholarship-program/scholarship-committee

United Nations. (1948). *Universal declaration of human rights (UDHR)*. https://www.un.org/en/about-us/universal-declaration-of-human-rights

University of Waterloo. (1968). *The Coryphaeus*. University of Waterloo.

Von Zur-Muehlen, M. (1983). The changing profile of full-time faculty at Canadian universities. *Canadian Journal of Higher Education*, *13*(2), 27–40. https://doi.org/10.47678/cjhe.v13i2.182894

Waterloo Region Record. (2021, March 26). *Dr Leonard P. Fletcher: 1927–2021*. https://www.legacy.com/ca/obituaries/therecord-waterloo/name/leonard-fletcher-obituary?id=40413070

Part II

New Ways Forward

Chapter 7

New Ways Forward: Black-First *Praxis*

Introduction

In this post-Negro-Apocalypse world, it is crucial that we utilize theoretical and practical frameworks *(praxis)* that centre on past, present and future means for Black Liberation. As I have written in this book, the Negro-Apocalypse is the period that mainstream media outlets referred to as the 'racial awakening' of post-25 May 2020. The period before EDI and DEI became DIE; the period before racist policies and legislations across North America restricted the teachings, hiring and promotion of 'inclusive' workplace and educational practices and procedures. One may argue that 2020 to 2023 was akin to the 1865 to 1877 period of Reconstruction in the United States (US). There were many reforms to support and 'uplift' Black people following the end of enslavement in the country. Using this historical lens, the rise of the KKK and lynching at the turn of the 20th century were the B(l)acklash when laws no longer could keep Black people in their 'place'. One might also argue that ICE, para-military police budgets and right-wing leaders are the 21st century parallels. We now find ourselves in the epoch of epistemic violence; this is a period of time where we have Apartheid, Jim Crow, colonialism and early twentieth-century fascism, all bundled up nicely on our social media feeds.

This chapter examines why traditional frameworks like DEI have failed to deliver liberation and argues for a Black-first *praxis* rooted in historical knowledge, cultural resistance and futurist thinking. This chapter builds on the case study of the global influences of Black inclusion and exclusion through the Canadian university's role in the transnational movement of Black (student) bodies. By revisiting lessons from past struggles, exploring cultural expressions such as soca and Afrofuturism, and interrogating systemic structures through sport and economics, we chart new ways forward for Black Liberation that are explored in Part II of this book, and in the 21st century at large.

Unmasking DEI, 107–117

doi:10.1108/978-1-83708-356-520261007

From DEI to Black-First *Praxis*: Why Existing Systems Fail

There are many who are grieving and lamenting our current state of affairs. They are genuinely baffled by the fact that DEI did not work, that DEI could work, that DEI *should* work. I actually hear that mostly from White moderates (and when I refer to White moderates, I am not referring to White people per se, but the treasure trove of non-White people that have adopted the belief that achieving and/or aspiring to Whiteness will solve all of life's problems). These are the 'well-meaning' neoliberals that believe that if you work hard, you will succeed; the 'buy-a-suit' and 'cut-your-dreads' types. They genuinely ask, 'How did we get here?' I challenge them to look to our histories. Fanon warned us. Dr King warned us. Assata warned us. So why are some so dismayed and disillusioned by the banning of the books, the closing of DEI offices, the firing/resignations of Black leaders in PWIs? This has happened before, and it will happen again. The long road of hegemonic oppression rests on the principles of change and continuity; have a generation believe a structural change is afoot, meanwhile the ominous and omnipresent cloud of shape shifting coercion and domination maintains its boot on your neck. There is a reason why they are banning critical race theory (CRT) and refuse to mandate the teachings of Black history across Ontario and North America; once we learn the truth, we can move forward.

Learning From History: Continuity and Change in Black Liberation

We, as Black people, cannot rely on existing systems that have proven to work to our detriment. We know the histories of DEI across the Black Atlantic. The laws and policies, particularly in Canada, have existed since 1774. Black people were 'free' in England since 1772, the legislated dehumanization ended in the US in 1865. CRT came to be in the 1960s precisely to prove that these benevolent changes simply masked a more devious form of anti-Black racism, like the silent killer of carbon monoxide; one that you cannot feel, touch, taste or prove, but is as deadly as ever.

We need to pivot. We need to understand that Black existence and resistance did not begin in 2020. We must look to the past. We must engage with the words and wisdom of our Griots, ancestors and elders. We must engage with our pre-colonial, pre-enslavement and anti-colonial ways of being. We must not dismiss or pacify the unwritten and silenced voices of our kin on the bottom of the Atlantic, the ones whose resistance meant the self-actualization of their own deaths so that we could live. We must not ridicule or pathologize our dehumanized siblings that toiled on plantations for cubes of sugar in English tea. We must move in unison to the beats of our outlawed drums as we fought for our emancipation. We must reflect on our contradictory blessings of illiteracy and literacy under neo-colonial machinations. We must replicate the fortitude of our freedom fighters of 1627, 1816, 1834, 1937, 1966 and 2021. We must continue to learn from the women of 1955, and the students of 1969, the youth of 1992. We must be wary of the promises of 25 May 2020.

Our liberation is predicated on our understanding of 'Black-first' ways of living our lives. DEI won't save us. The question is, how do we define this concept of liberation? How do we define *Black* liberation? In academic, non-academic and professional spaces, I believe that we must move beyond the restrictive structures of traditional disciplines and models that do not necessarily work for us. I say that these systems 'do not necessarily work' as the enslavement and oppression of many has facilitated the liberation for some. 'Race', 'racism' and 'Blackness', as this book has highlighted, are tools designed to reduce a group of imagined peoples to a *thing*, an object, some *thing* that was deemed to be worth less. Black liberation must understand the roots of oppression, without falling victim to its shape shifting power of making bread crumbs of progress seem like a five-course meal. This is where one must move with caution throughout this unmasked space of DEI; a space that reifies race logics without properly interrogating the institutionalized and ominous presence of race and racism as founding principles of our society. One cannot liberate with a myopic view that DEI, a framework designed to appease and assuage but never liberate, will be the Ark that takes us to the Promised Land. As Frantz Fanon (1956) stated, 'a people that undertakes a struggle for liberation rarely legitimizes race prejudice' (p. 131). That being said, we must not legitimize race prejudice, but we also must not ignore it. Nor can we fall into the trap of believing that individualized race prejudice can be fixed by the 'I' in 'DEI' – simply including and integrating oppressed people into PWIs (organizations, schools, corporations, etc.) that were fundamentally designed to exclude and marginalize their very existence. We must also have ability to understand the purpose of these systems to fundamentally engage with how the 'I' was, and is, meant to perpetuate their unmitigated growth.

Thinking in Systems in a 'Me-First' Society: Learning From Our Plantocracy Past

Donella H. Meadows (2008) in *Thinking in Systems: A Primer* argued, 'An important function of almost every system is to ensure its own perpetuation' (p. 15). Meadows (2008) understands this system as, 'an interconnected set of elements that is coherently organized in a way that achieves something... a system must consist three kinds of things: *elements*, *interconnections* and a *function* or *purpose*' (p. 11, emphasis in original). The author uses the example of a sports team to highlight the function of a system:

> A football team is a system with elements such as players, coach, field and ball. Its interconnections are the rules of the game, the coach's strategy, the players' communications and the laws of physics that govern the motions of ball and players. The purpose of the team is to win games, or have fun, or get exercise, or make millions of dollars, or all of the above. (p. 11)

This may seem like fun and games, but what if this sport of football is really a business in the throes of capitalism? That the only purpose of the people that own the teams is to make money off the tried and true process of using Black bodies? There can be more Black bodies on the pitch (in the United Kingdom) or the field (in North America) that make millions of dollars, but what if their labour (and bodies) is expendable? What if their Self is tied to the purpose of the 21st century plantocracy? What is fundamentally different from what Eric Williams wrote in 1944 about the system of 'Negro Slavery', which 'therefore was only a solution, in certain historical circumstances, of the Caribbean labour problem' (p. 29)? In this instance, the 'football game' took place on sugar plantations, and its players (Black) Caribbean labourers. Williams (1944) argued:

> The emancipation of the Negro and the inadequacy of the White worker put the sugar planter back to where he had been in the seventeenth century. He still needed labour. Then he had moved from Indian (Indigenous) to White to Negro. Now, deprived of his Negro, he turned back to White and then to Indian, this time the Indian from the East. (p. 28)

This is important to note, as Williams (1944) stated, 'the abolition of slavery did not mean the destruction of the sugar plantation' (p. 28). Rather, it created a state in the early 19th century where, 'the Negroes had been stimulated to freedom by the development of the very wealth which their labour had created' (Williams, 1944, p. 208). I believe that these historical lessons and frameworks have been lost in the language of 21st century DEI practitioners. Black liberation, its successes, failures and contradictions, have real applications in our present-day realities.

Though the 'colour' of the elements may have changed, the purpose of the system (sugar plantations) remained the same: to create wealth by exploiting labour. Once we conflate Williams' framework with the histories and mythologies of White supremacy, Nathaniel Bacon, Windrush, civil and human rights movements, Black Atlantic immigration policies and the omnipresent language of DEI in the 21st century, we can begin to see a similar pattern of Black oppression and exploitation. The change and continuity of the Black condition is subject to the changing tides of the Atlantic. However, these lessons, along with a revisiting of pre-eminent thinkers that studied systems of Black enslavement such as Eric Williams, we can find foundational answers to our liberation. The legalized and economic 'freedom' from enslavement was 'an attack on monopoly. Their opponents were not only the humanitarians but the capitalists' (Williams, 1944, p. 135). In a lesser-known twist of fate, Black people sat on the tip of the double-edged sword of capitalism: their labour precipitated the Trade, but also stood as a barrier to free markets. As Williams (1944) wrote, 'the capitalists had first encouraged West Indian slavery and then helped to destroy it' (p. 169). What we must understand is that 'freedom' was not a benevolent action to support Black humanization – it was driven by economic factors. Money drives the interest convergence of White support for the Black condition. Black communities must pivot away from these reluctantly given freedoms that are 'given' to us from White supremacist rulers: often with conditions; often, and quickly, taken away at the drop of a social media post; often, just 'words' that make the ruling class look 'progressive'. We must move towards a more substantive and autonomous freedom.

Cultural Resistance as *Praxis*: Soca, Carnival and the African Personality

You can feel it on your blood. In your soul. You can *feel* the freedom on the streets for Crop Over, Carnival, Spicemas, Caribana, Notting Hill and other festivals around the Caribbean and globally. *We* can feel the sweet sounds of liberation, but soca is simply perceived as happy 'jump up' music, often devoid of its original emancipatory ethos. I argue that soca music is analogous to the proliferation of reggae music as a vector for Rastafari, Black consciousness and the African Personality. The post-colonial Ghanaian diplomat, Alex Quaison-Sackey, postulated on the concept of African Personality and its relationship to Pan-Africanism in his 1963 book, *Africa Unbound: Reflections of an African Statesman*. He stated that the African Personality is the 'the cultural expression of what is common to all peoples whose home is on the continent of Africa', and it 'projects a figure of action and thought, of unified power, which displays itself, and thereby defines itself, in action – particularly political action. . .it is so closely related to other political ideas such as Pan-Africanism' (Quaison-Sackey, 1963, p. 36, 37). The emphasis must be placed on the convergence of cultural identity and political action. Quaison-Sackey (1963) wrote, 'The African knows that he must emerge not only politically but psychologically as well' (p. 40).

The ethos of the 'indigenous African' was incompatible with domination and colonization. Its essence of humanization equated to freedom. This is highlighted by Aimé Césaire's (1939/2013) manifestation of *Négritude*, and Senegalese president Léopold Senghor's amplification of a politicized cultural acceptance, affirmation and proliferation of Black pride across the Diaspora and the Continent. Grounded in French speaking Black nations, Négritude was the foundation for Black consciousness across the Diaspora. Quaison-Sackey (1963) affirms these assertions, writing:

> For in attempting to rid his continent of foreign and colonial domination, the African is attempting nothing less than the ultimate recapture and reassertion of the dignity of the individual – a dignity which the colonial system attempted to reduce and, in some cases, to exterminate altogether. (p. 37)

Liberation has long equated to self-pride, self-love and Black cultural expression.

Soca music expounds and highlights the deep and intricate humanization of Black peoples as characterized by the pursuit for emancipation and liberation. As

Frantz Fanon (1964/1967) states in *Towards the African Revolution: Political Essays*, 'The process of liberation of man, independently of the concrete situations in which he finds himself, includes and concerns the whole of humanity' (p. 144). In other words, and again, liberation means humanization. The Transatlantic Slave Trade and the process of enslavement dehumanized darker-skinned peoples from the African Continent. To liberate, then, meant to 'return' to the African Personality and to humanize one's Self. Some may argue that one can never 'fully' return, but consciously mitigate and integrate colonial ways of being through a hegemonic 'reversion' to African ways of being. In simpler terms, it is effectively a Creolized African Personality – you may not have been born in Africa or 'go back' to the Continent, but African ways of being are born in you. They manifest in your day-to-day means of survival in oppressive spaces. It meant to love one's creolized phenotype in the Americas. Fanon (1964) argues that it is 'the colonial peoples who must liberate themselves from colonialist domination', as 'Colonialism is not a type of individual relations but the conquest of a national territory and the oppression of a people: that is all' (p. 81, 105). He continued, 'The struggle of the inferiorized is situated on a markedly more human level. The perspectives are radically new. The opposition is the henceforth classical one of the struggles of conquest and of liberation' (Fanon, 1964, p. 43). Colonialism relates to the dehumanization of the subaltern. Soca music and its ties to Caribbean carnival festivals such as Crop Over and Carnival, are an everyday form of resistance. We must take into account the frameworks of Afrofuturism and, similarly, the words of Rinaldo Walcott (2021) who writes that 'abolition wasn't something of the past: it was an ongoing, contemporary movement, that would not be over until Black people everywhere were free, equal and safe' (p. 10). We (Black people) are still colonial beings – soca music is *uMkhonto we Sizwe* (the spear of the nation) of accessible Black liberation and emancipation; a tool by which we must encompass lessons of Black pasts, present and futures. As Black-first *praxis*, soca allows Black people to come together and emancipate as we 'pelt waist' alongside our ancestors. Afrofuturism, as I explain in the next section, allows us to imagine all possibilities that seemed too far out of reach in this context across time and space.

Imagining Liberated Futures: Afrofuturism and Revolutionary Thought

The Smithsonian's National Museum of African American History and Culture exhibit, 'Afrofuturism: A History of Black Futures', described how Afrofuturism 'expresses notions of Black identity, agency and freedom through art, creative works and activism that envision liberated futures for Black life' (Smithsonian, n.d., para. 3). London, England's Tate Museum states that 'Afrofuturism is a cultural aesthetic that combines science-fiction, history and fantasy to explore the African-American experience and aims to connect those from the black diaspora with their forgotten African ancestry' (Tate, n.d., para. 1). Afrofuturist elders, particularly the iconic Octavia E. Butler, emerged as 'a powerful voice in science fiction in the 1970s… [featuring] Black female protagonists challenging hierarchies of race, class and gender' (Smithsonian, n.d., para. 7). She created her own fields and narratives with Black stories with Black characters that did not fall into of what Walker (1997) argued were the 'five 'orientations' in African-Canadian historiography' (p. 166). While the term Afrofuturism is rooted in science fiction, it is its 'otherness that is at the heart of afrofuturism', as it is 'generally used to refer to literature, music and visual art that explores the African-American experience and in particular the role of slavery in that experience' (Tate, n.d., para. 2, 3). Michael Bennett (2016) states Afrofuturism is 'new plausible social arrangements, political structures and technological systems, Afrofuturism estranges its viewership from the belief that life must be as it currently is' (p. 92). He continues; 'The best of Afrofuturism is vibrantly rich, deeply evocative and intensely polyvocal and multimodal', as it is 'capable of rescuing its viewership from idolatrous commitments to false necessities' (Bennett, 2016, p. 92). The author highlights three leading voices on Afrofuturism, Ytasha Womack, Alondra Nelson and Mark Dery; all have described Afrofuturism as encompassing critical, artistic and cultural works including science fiction, technology and non-Western beliefs with a futurist orientation (Bennett, 2016). Bennett (2016) argued that the Afro-futurists 'often focus on appropriating and redeploying technological devices or scientific knowledge and on both raising and razing the consciousness of people from the African diaspora' (p. 92). Afrofuturism is our liberated future.

It is important that one comprehends that Afrofuturism, or futurist framework for Black Liberation, is rooted in history. Bennett (2016) contended that W.E.B. DuBois' articulation of Black double-consciousness and Black ontologies are 'remixed and recomplicated in Afrofuturism – its byproduct is *nth-order* consciousness' (p. 93, emphasis in original). I contend that a close reading and understanding of Black historical events is quintessential to Black Liberation to inform future movements and revolutionary frameworks. The Afrofuturist takes this approach one step further as their works challenge and reinterpret histories of Black oppression. Bennett (2016) stated how Afrofuturists 'often reconfigure the Atlantic slave trade as an alien abduction or the conversion of humans into technology, quintessential elements of science fiction' (p. 93). Slavery was not a static characterization, nor was enslavement a temporal social, political and economic condition: for the enslaved, slavery, was 'akin to that of the classic science fiction concept of apocalypse, viscerally describing what it feels like to live through catastrophe' (Bennett, 2016, p. 93). The Militant Millennial – the Black youth unapologetically pushing for change in our contemporary society – must firmly recognize that their present-day condition, both positive and negative, is rooted in historical machinations. For those in the Black Atlantic, the Transatlantic Slave Trade and enslavement was the singular most destructive 'event' with its ominous tentacles of deceit, ideological and through legislation.

Afrofuturism as a Means to Move Forward by Engaging With Our Traumatic Past to Create a Better Future

Jean-Pierre Bekolo (2023) expands the African-American centric and enslavement framework and situates Afrofuturism as a critique of the colonial past and neo-colonial present of the Continent. He states that the 'present is sometimes a prison. When it becomes impossible to imagine anything other than this present you live in. Many Africans tend to cherish this place where the White man left us' (Bekolo, 2023, p. 380). Writing on Frantz Fanon, Bekolo (2023) continues, noting that:

> He saw the world as a sick place and humans as people to be healed. This is what an intellectual must do, at least in Africa. Instead of 'instructing', we must 'build', or reconstruct with what we have and what we are, the world we want. (p. 383)

Understanding Fanon's work on Black mental health and psychology, the author stated that it 'is easier for the filmmaker to be an intellectual therapist because he or she works with a medium that can reproduce the world and life' (Bekolo, 2023, p. 383). I challenge this and state that all those involved in Black liberation movements should, and must, build upon the efforts of our Emigrant Ambassador elders and collate our expertise that all of our media can reproduce the world and life. Our efforts must have defined purpose to liberate.

What interests me, particularly in this post-Negro-Apocalypse environment, is for this generation of Militant Millennials liberators, to situate 25 May 2020 as our 1604, 1619 or 1627. What must we (un)learn from our current apocalyptic condition that we are not 'free' in the sense that the wider society has made us believe in the 2020s. That the change and continuity of our enslaved conditions persists; however, we are required to scaffold the learnings of past apocalyptic and post-apocalyptic liberation movements of the past. Instead of writing and curating works as an alternate reality rooted in the arts or science fiction, I challenge 'mainstream' scholars to use the language of Afrofuturists, specifically as it relates to historical and present-day Black conditions. Articulate to the masses of what it meant to live through the Negro-Apocalypse of the 2020s, and whether it is desirable to continue to live this way or rather choose a different path or orientation. We need an Afrofuturist orientation, emboldened by other Black-first *praxis* frameworks.

Sport and the Politics of Black Labour: Lessons From the Field

The NBA Ain't It

I think back to a conversation I had with someone during the pandemic as it related to the NBA and its response to the murder of George Floyd. I said that if all the Black stars in the NBA at the time (e.g. LeBron James, Kevin Durant, Stephen Curry) decided to remove their (Black) labour and stop playing in the NBA, they could/should have ended the NBA. This isn't to say that their professional basketball careers would take a hit; they undoubtedly would. However, they have enough capital and interest from sponsors and fans to create their own leagues and dictate how their labour would be (ab)used. This idea is not novel, particularly in sport, nor is it novel in academia, business or politics. The call for 'Black-owned' or 'Black-supported' spaces is generational. When it comes to sport, we can look to the pages of William C. Rhoden's (2006) *Forty Million Dollar Slaves: The Rise, Fall, and Redemption of the Black Athlete* chronicling the Black athletes on the foreground of American culture. Rhoden (2006) writes:

> Black athletes have symbolically carried the weight of a race's eternal burden of proof; their performances were among the most visible evidences that [B]lacks, as a community, were good enough, smart enough, strong enough, brave enough – indeed, human enough – to share in the fruits of this nation with full citizenship and humanity. (p. 3, emphasis in original)

In this space of oppression, one that I argue extends far beyond the boundaries of the US and swept across the Black Atlantic, created an environment where Black people were given lemons and grew lemon orchards. Rhoden (2006) wrote, 'When segregation became the law of the land, power meant creating our own institutions, like Rube Foster's Negro Leagues, which created economies around sport and allowed for the development of a uniquely [B]lack athletic style' (p. 6). *Fire in Babylon* (Riley, 2010) is the legacy artefact that captures the sheer dominance of West Indies cricket in 1970s and 1980s – Black Brits, the sons of enslaved people, dominating (i.e. striking fear) into the hearts of their former massas and colonial overseers at their own sport, a sport used to colonize and control. While this example is not the same as creating their own league, you can argue that 'beating them at their own game' holds more power than anything else does. It would be the equivalent of taking the DEI structure and creating Black-first businesses and institutions, while bowling indiscriminate and vicious bouncers at the heads of your former (White) bosses.

Explaining the Limits of DEI Through Jockey Syndrome: Changing the Rules Once We 'Get Ahead'

We need to take another example from sport to understand the changing yardsticks of DEI. We are always left wondering how we can never seemingly get ahead as a Black Collective, when on the surface, DEI policies and initiatives seem to have everything that it takes to help us move forward. Rhoden used the historical example of Black jockey dominance in the US during the late 18th to the early 20th centuries. Rhoden (2006) writes that the Jockey Syndrome is:

> changing the rules to fit a need – the need to maintain control in the face of a perceived challenge to White supremacy. The Jockey Syndrome is distinguished by a changing of the rules of the game when competition begins to gain ground. It usually involves a series of manoeuvres to facilitate racist outcomes, including the taking away of previously granted rights and the diluting of access through coercive power and force, a phenomenon that was common outside of sports as well, of course. Black Americans

> would see that clearly in the Civil Rights Act they celebrated in 1875 was almost completely overturned by the Plessy v. Ferguson case of 1896. (p. 68)

DEI was to be the solution to the 'racial awakening' of the 2020s, but ultimately became a symptom of the Negro-Apocalypse. The Oppressor, quicker than ever this time, saw that the Black jockeys were (allegedly) gaining ground against the dominant power structures. In reality, most of those gains were performative, only reinforcing the neoliberal individualism of 'me-first' and 'me-only' society. The rules of the game needed to be changed. DEI needed to reflect an attack against White people and their way of life.

Conclusion: A Way Forward

In sum, this chapter argues that liberation cannot emerge from frameworks designed to maintain systemic power. By centring Black-first *praxis*, grounded in historical lessons, cultural resistance and futurist visions, we move beyond performative inclusion towards genuine emancipation. The key, as I argue with the ideological tenets of DEI in the 21st century, is to create the illusion of freedom to continue to exploit and subjugate under the guise of 'improved' conditions. Moreover, it is paramount that the exploited believe in their freedom and will consequently 'buy-in' to these neoliberal thoughts of social mobility. There is the belief that you can succeed if you 'buy-in' to the auspices of diversity, equity and inclusion. Meanwhile, the twenty-first-century plantocracy, or the Oligarchs, or the 1 percenters, or the PWIs, or whatever term we decide to use for those with institutional power in the 2020s and beyond, give us piecemeal handouts to appease as they continue unfettered ways to maintain their systems with little to no opposition. The path forward demands that we dismantle these illusions of progress and build systems rooted in Black ways of knowing, being and thriving. We must engage with these historical Black thinkers, both those who are scholarly and published and those who have not but live Black liberation through their work, to be able to see and understand our historical, political and social standing and Self in oppressive spaces. Only then can we truly overstand the words of Robert Nesta Marley (1980) and 'emancipate ourselves from mental slavery' (1:14).

As we close this chapter on Black-first *praxis* and the imperative to move beyond appeasement frameworks, we turn to a historical case study that grounds these ideas in lived experience. Barbados offers a blueprint for liberation forged through rebellion, labour movements and transnational solidarities. Chapter 8 examines how these struggles illuminate both the possibilities and contradictions of emancipation, and how their lessons can inform our present fight against systemic anti-Blackness.

References

Bekolo, J. (2023). Afrofuturism. *The Comparatist*, *47*, 379–388. https://doi.org/10.1353/com.2023.a911949

Bennett, M. (2016). Afrofuturism. *Computer*, *49*(4), 92–93. https://doi.org/10.1109/MC.2016.99

Césaire, A. (2013). The original 1939 notebook of a return to the native land. In A. J. Arnold & C. Eshleman (Eds.), *Weslayan*. (Originally published in 1939).

Fanon, F. (1956). Racism and culture. *Presence Africaine: Cultural Journal of the Negro World*, *8/10*, 122–131. https://www.freedomarchives.org/Documents/Finder/Black%20Liberation%20Disk/Black%20Power!/SugahData/Journals/Presence.S.pdf

Fanon, F. (1964/1967). *Toward the African revolution: Political essays* (H. Chevalier, Trans.). Grove Press.

Marley, R. N. [Bob Marley and the Wailers]. (1980). Redemption song [Song]. In *On Uprising* [Album]. Island.

Meadows, D. H. (2008). *Thinking in systems: A primer*. Chelsea Green Publishing.

Quaison-Sackey, A. (1963). *Africa unbound: Reflections of an African statesman*. Frederick A. Praeger.

Rhoden, W. C. (2006). *Forty million dollar slaves: The rise, fall, and redemption of the Black athlete*. Three Rivers Press.

Smithsonian. (n.d.). *Afrofuturism: A history of Black futures*. National Museum of African American History & Culture. https://nmaahc.si.edu/explore/exhibitions/afrofuturism

Smithsonian. (n.d.). *Five you should know: Black women icons of Afrofuturism*. African American History & Culture. https://nmaahc.si.edu/explore/stories/five-you-should-know-black-women-icons-afrofuturism

Tate. (n.d.). *Afrofuturism*. Tate Gallery. https://www.tate.org.uk/art/art-terms/a/afrofuturism

Walker, J. W. S. G. (1997). Allegories and orientations in African-Canadian historiography: The spirit of Africville. *Dalhousie Review*, *77*(2), 155–177. http://hdl.handle.net/10222/63274

Williams, E. (1944). *Capitalism & slavery*. The University of North Carolina Press.

Chapter 8

Barbados as a Model for Liberation

Introduction: Barbados and the Search for Liberation

In the search for 'new' Black liberation *praxis*, Barbados' Black liberation and emancipatory struggles of the 19th and early 20th century are notable. They have been key guiding frameworks for me as I have navigated the professional roadblocks of DEI spoken about throughout this book. Often referred to by the moniker 'Little England,' the White supremacist educational and political structures embedded on the Island have sanitized its connection to global Black Liberation struggles, but they exist and are deeply embedded in the coral foundations of Barbados. We must critically engage with the intersectional historical forces: violent abolitionary movements, Black Zionism and politicized Black and proletariat-led labour movements. Critically engaging with these movements contextualizes the conceptualizations of Barbados and the ways that the Island is influenced, or is not, by the hegemonic power of British colonization, including the ways that colonialism remains embedded in Barbadian plantocracies and edutocracy.

Building on Chapter 7's call for Black-first *praxis*, this chapter turns to Barbados as a living archive of liberation. From the Bussa Rebellion to twentieth-century labour uprisings, Barbados offers critical lessons on resistance, adaptation and empowerment. By examining these movements alongside the island's educational structures and transnational connections, we uncover how historical frameworks can inform present-day strategies for dismantling systemic oppression and reimagining DEI beyond performative inclusion.

Historical Foundations of Resistance: The Bussa Rebellion and Beyond

The Bussa Rebellion of Easter 1816 in Barbados was caused by the 'rumour' of emancipation on 1 January 1816. The 'whole was strengthened by the information, imported by some free People of Colour', and by enslaved peoples 'who

Unmasking DEI, 119–126

doi:10.1108/978-1-83708-356-520261008

had gained an ascendancy over their fellows by being enabled to read and write' (Barbados House of Assembly [BHA], 1818, p. 6). The slave revolt began, 'by many of the leading Slaves (directed and encouraged by a few Free People of Colour)', as the 'nearer approximation which existed between the Free People of Colour and Slaves, arising frequently from original connection or previous acquaintance' facilitated the exchange of revolutionary ideas (BHA, 1818, p. 8, 11). King Wiltshire, an enslaved person belonging to the Bayley's Plantation in Barbados, drew attention to the role the image of the Black woman played in the rebellion. Wiltshire testified that:

> the negroes were to be freed, and that their freedom was to be given them through a [B]lack woman who was a Queen, for whom Wilberforce acted in England: that some free coloured men, namely, Cain Davis, Roach and Sarjeant, had told him this. (BHA, 1818, p. 27)

Women at the Forefront: Nanny Grigg, Errol Barrow, and Revolutionary Ideology

Nanny Grigg, a Black woman at the forefront of the Bussa Rebellion, was characterized as a 'revolutionary ideologue' (Beckles, 1998, p. 46). The Barbados Assembly's official 1818 report described Grigg as a 'literate, knowledgeable woman who believed and propagated the view that in order to secure freedom it was possible to replicate the Haitian Revolution' (as cited in Beckles, 1998, p. 46).

In his address to the Barbados Constitutional Conference in London, July 1966, 'No loitering on colonial premises', the soon to be Prime Minister of Barbados, Sir Errol Walton Barrow, rooted Barbados independent ideals to the early 17th century. He stated:

> when in 1639 your own country had been governed without a Parliament for 11 years, the English inhabitants of Barbados settled a Parliament for themselves and thereby created the Legislative institutions which we have since, without any disturbance enjoyed. In this respect, Barbados shared only with Virginia, Massachusetts and Bermuda, the solid comforts of representative government. (Barrow, 1966, p. 87)

He highlighted the signing of the 1651 Charter of Barbados as an example of Barbadian independence from the metropole. He argued that Barbados had over 300 years to prepare for independence:

> Three centuries of history answer that question in the affirmative. You have never had to shore up our finances; you have never had

> to maintain or preserve public order among us. Even now, without the help of our best citizens, your own hospital and transport system would be in jeopardy. (Barrow, 1966, p. 89)

Political Mobilization and Labour Movements: Clement Payne and the 1937 Uprising

Referring to the 1937 Rebellion in Barbados, Barrow stated, 'The Westindies (sic), apart from the cricket field, first came into prominence because the ordinary men and women in the street, and not any political leader, decided to revolt and rebel against those conditions'. I argue that one of these forgotten 'ordinary men' was Clement Payne. The Right Excellent Clement Osbourne Payne was a Trinidadian-born, National Hero of Barbados (National Cultural Foundation [NCF], 2021). The young political revolutionary preached of non-violence and galvanized the Black working-class spirit to 'remember to keep the lights always burning, continue to hold mass meetings, Organize, Educate, Agitate, but do not violate'. Under the backdrop of a global depression, working-class uprisings throughout the West Indies (particularly in Trinidad), and conservative national newspaper journalism and its 'HUSH-HUSH' policy, Payne agitated against the repressive forces of the (White) Barbadian plantocracy, the political elites and the Barbadian colonial police force. He founded the Barbados Progressive Workingmen's Association. For his political action, he was served with an Order of Expulsion. Barbadian authorities shipped him to his birthplace of Trinidad (Comissiong, 2021).

Once the working-class masses learned of his deportation, Payne's 'non-violent' philosophy dissipated quickly. His deportation 'proved to be the catalyst for an eruption of all the pent up anger, frustration and bitterness created by centuries of slavery, oppression and victimization in Barbados' (Comissiong, 2021, p. 18). In the four days of countrywide rebellion against ideological and institutional White supremacy in 1937, 14 people lost their lives and 47 were wounded, 500 people were detained and arrested, and Barbados suffered millions of dollars of damage to physical property (NCF, 2021). Payne never returned to Barbados and died of an apparent heart attack in 1941 (NCF, 2021). Through the political mobilization and organization of the Black working class and the People's Uprising of 1937, several political and societal changes came to bear. These included, but are not limited to: the establishment of the Barbados Labour Party and the Congress Party; trade unions, including the Barbados Workers Union; creation and enactment of the *Trade Union Act* of 1940; Women's suffrage in 1944; Universal Adult Suffrage in 1950; the outlawing of child labour; penal reform; and the establishment of a Director of Education (Comissiong, 2021). Payne and then events of 1937 highlight the real outcomes of Black collective bodies and minds, agitated by internal discontent and lived realities, and supported by transnational and international working class and Black solidarity movements.

Transnational Connections: Garveyism, Pan-Africanism and Global Solidarity

One must note Payne's connection to the Universal Negro Improvement Association (UNIA), and Barbados' broader transnational engagement with Black liberation. In his 'My Political Memoirs of Barbados', Payne stated that he was 'attracted by the activities of the Universal Negro Improvement Association, where I was privileged to make my first public appearance and addressed a composite audience of about three hundred persons' (Comissiong, 2021, p. 5). While steeped in precarious, and arguably detrimental patriarchal and neo-colonial values, Marcus Garvey's early twentieth-century UNIA emphasis on 'self-help' and Black Pride encouraged 'international ties with [B]lacks in Great Britain, the West Indies, Central America and the United States' (Mathieu, 2010, p. 156). Garvey, a born Jamaican, was one of the most influential leaders of Pan-Africanism in the early 1900s. He inspired the likes of countless leaders throughout the Black Atlantic, and his messages of the Pan-Africanism and Pan-African belief in the 'unity, common history and common purpose of the peoples of Africa and the African diaspora and the notion that their destinies are interconnected' (Adi, 2018, p. 2). This includes the 'importance of then liberation and advancement of the African continent itself, not just for its inhabitants, but also as the homeland of the entire African diaspora' (Adi, 2018, p. 2).

Garvey was not, and should not, be matriculated as the protagonist of Black liberation in the 20th century; however, it is undeniable that the West Indies and the broader Caribbean archipelago was, and is, a central site for Black resistance, agitation and liberation. This includes, but is not limited to, such figures and events as: the struggle for Dayiti (i.e. the Haitian Revolution), Toussaint Louverture, Jean-Jacques Dessalines; Nanny of the Maroons and other Maroon communities in Jamaica; Trinidadian-born Kwame Ture/Stokely Carmichael, the Student Nonviolent Coordinating Committee (SNCC) and the Black Panther Party for Self-Defence; Malcolm X, who was inspired by the UNIA and whose mother was born in the Caribbean; Guyanese intellectual Walter Rodney; Trinidadian Eric Williams; and currently the such global figures as Barbados' Prime Minister, Mia Mottley. The Caribbean, and Barbados in particular, must be recognized as the 'original sin' of Black enslaved societies, while simultaneously serving as the foundation for Black democracies, liberation and emancipation.

Liberation and Contradictions: The 'Back to Africa' Movements and Black Elitism

With this recognition, however, scholars and Black liberators in the 21st century must continue to problematize the ideologies and histories of unity, progress and liberation through subjugation. Pivoting the access of understanding of collective 'Blackness' away from an African-American (United States of America)-centric area of focus allows for more transnational critiques of these movements. This includes the 'creation' of Liberia as a 'state held together by [B]lackness' (Banton, 2019, p. 1) and the role Bajans played in reinforcing heterogeneous and reified divisions around the social, political and historical creation of Blackness. With respect to the founding of Liberia, Caree A. Banton (2019) argued that '[B]lackness was as much a colour as it was an unsteady idea' (p. 4). Moreover, colonialism and neo-colonialism exemplified 'Back to Africa' movements of the 19th and 20th centuries. The concept of 'Black Freedom' predicated Black subjugation and was present in the philosophies and operationalization of the American Colonization Society, Martin Delaney, Garvey, the creation of Sierra Leone and Liberia. As Banton (2019) stated, 'Some [B]lack migrants had not rejected oppression but rather showed a predilection of the sort of [B]lack particularity and ethnocentrism imbued with the kinds of authoritarianism that benefited them' (p. 4). A select number of 'privileged' 19th century Bajans participated in a colonial project where the 'maintenance of previous power structures only benefited and valorized some groups of [B]lacks, and forced others to assimilate or be excluded' (Banton, 2019, p. 4). Black Bajan 'elitism' and the attempt to deconstruct institutional White power structures simultaneously contributed to the reinforcement of race-based societal stratifications.

In the conversation surrounding DEI, this historical understanding is critically important. There are quite a few people that question why some Black people would openly decide to 'sell-out' and 'fit-in' to a system that could, and would, deliberately make them sell their souls for a pay cheque. People may call them 'tokens;' I would call myself Dr Bojangles at times. A reference to the early twentieth-century Black tap dancer Bill 'Bojangles' Robinson. I would be out there dancing for massa with my best minstrel cap on to make sure they enjoyed the performative show of DEI. *Black skins with white masks*. However, the 'Back to Africa' examples provided here by Banton give us a bit of food for thought; maybe the (Black) people that spent decades of their lives trying to fit in in school, learning 'unaccented' English, going to university dorm parties, changing their 'ethnic sounding' names, buying the suits, learning how to use chop sticks, buying a Nutribullet, watching Friends and listening to Oasis, contributing to the office potluck with a tuna casserole, letting co-workers touch their hair, constantly being overlooked for a promotion and then having to train their new boss, or just constantly being made to feel lesser than, just want a chance to breathe and be seen and recognized. Maybe they have an intrinsic understanding of their value and worth, that they are Black Kings and Queens who are worthy of becoming the kind of person that DEI promises they will be. Can we fault them for wanting to dive head-first into the Kool-Aid of DEI? Yes, their post-2020 success may be seen as being built through the prism of DEI, but if it was a level-playing field, watching a man die for 8 minutes and 46 seconds would not have been needed to catalyse it in the first place.

Education as a Double-Edged Sword: Edutocracy and Colonial Legacies

As Kerry Ann Rockquemore and Tracy Laszloffy (2008) write in *The Black Academic's Guide to Winning Tenure – Without Losing Your Soul*, Black people who accept the DEI model, are using it as 'the feigned subservience habit of survival' (p. 131). This means that Black people in these PWIs 'assume a fake one-down or deferential stance in response to oppression' (Rockquemore & Laszloffy, 2008, p. 131). The authors use this as an example: 'It is not safe to openly resist oppression, so I will pretend to accept things the way they are while covertly resisting at all times' (Rockquemore & Laszloffy, 2008, p. 131). Black skins with (removable) White masks. In my own life and career, I have framed this as having a shadow strategy. In 2020 and 2021, everyone jumped on the DEI bandwagon. I knew very well that this was a fleeting moment, so I put in as much Black infrastructure (e.g. Black hires, Black scholarships, Black student supports) as possible, so when society inevitably pulled the plug on DEI, the changes I wanted were already baked into the system. Then, when the world came calling to end DEI, I 'feigned subservience' and went ahead with it with little resistance. Why? I already knew that I got what I wanted. Now I looked like the 'team player' that was supporting the cause (against DEI). DEI became the target, but the target became performative actions that did not, and would not, make the systemic changes needed to confront anti-Black racism. People would spend their energy against DEI since it was, and is, a polarizing term, but had little bandwidth to see that we were playing chess and they were playing checkers. Acceptance can be resistance.

We must engage with the understanding of the intersections of resistance, acceptance and adaption as a complex means of empowerment. An analogous framing of this argument is to engage with the histories of syncretic religions. One example is Umbanda, a 'religious compromise' originating in Brazil and spreading across the Americas as a means to re-centre Afro-centric spirituality outlawed by the White supremacist plantocracies along with pieces of Euro-Western religion to 'answer the needs' of the diverse population (Espírito Santo, 2017, p. 181). The Barbadian education system, which predicated most social movements in Barbados in the late 18th and 20th centuries, continues to be a point of contention. Barbados is one of the most literate nation-states in the world and created an enviable 'culture of education'; however, scholars and politicians alike contend that this emphasis on colonial and neo-colonial education structures are a detriment to Bajans and Barbadian society (Denny, 2021). This system reinforces a co-dependent satellite state that facilitates the class stratification and geopolitical 'Brain Drains' of 'educated' Black Bajans. The education system reproduces Black nation states as collective subalterns to the whims of the economic and capitalist dalliances of exploitative and Global North societies (Moore, 2022). Stacy L. Denny (2021), when analysing Barbados' education system, posits her theory of edutocracy, which 'speaks to how colonial, plantocratic ideology shapes attitudes towards the purpose of [West Indian] education; attitudes in turn influence policies that emerge as curriculum, inform teaching practice, and affect learning outcomes' (p. 11). It is, in particular in the West Indian context, a 'fusion of education and plantocracy to describe education officials at the highest decision-making levels who unquestioningly support plantocratic ideologies, policies and practices that promote deleterious policies like European monolingual education in predominantly bi/multidialectal Afro-WI speech communities' (Denny, 2021, p. 2).

Lessons for Today: Resistance, Adaptation and DEI

Citing the work of Laurette Bristol, Denny (2021) argues, 'edutocracy is shown as a theory of dependency on Western ideas, knowledge, services, systems and policies based on ideologies of intellectual hegemony, academic power and legitimacy of imperial knowledge' (p. 11). Acquiescence should not be misconstrued as an antonym for resistance; however, a myopic pursuit of (colonial) education simultaneously reinforced the plantocracy's caste system. Organized and Eurocentric educational structures, which were of course the *only* accepted structures, were the foundation for Black political leaders and the enfranchisement of the Black working class since Emancipation. Within an oppressive socioeconomic and political system, access to political elite structures such as education have become analogous to success and progress. This is similar to how 'freedom through oppression' operated, where political, ideological and structural subjugation of Black peoples on the African continent supported Black Bajan social mobility. I contend that Black scholars and Black liberators must continue the conversation on whether striving for the Eurocentric ideals of 'democracy' is compatible with 'true' Black liberation and emancipation.

Conclusion: Barbados as a Blueprint for Black-First *Praxis*

Barbados' history demonstrates that liberation is neither linear nor uncontested. From rebellions and labour movements, to educational reforms and transnational solidarities, the island's struggles reveal both the possibilities and pitfalls of emancipation. These lessons underscore the argument advanced in this chapter cannot rely on frameworks designed to maintain systemic power. Instead, we must draw on historical models like Barbados to craft Black-first strategies that resist, adapt and transform. In doing so, we move beyond performative inclusion towards genuine emancipation. Emancipation rooted in our histories, responsive to our present, and oriented towards liberated futures.

Barbados teaches us that liberation is never linear – it is contested, adaptive and deeply rooted in histories of resistance. Yet these histories also remind us that freedom has always been negotiated through struggle, often under conditions of violence. Chapter 9 builds on this insight by interrogating the concept of emancipatory violence. Not as indiscriminate force, but as a multidimensional response to systemic oppression. We ask: What does it mean to be truly free when the structures of anti-Blackness remain intact?

Driven by the strength of my family and Bajan-Canadian upbringing, I have always looked to my ancestors and the histories of the 166 square miles of Barbados as guiding posts to my (and our) continued liberation. The key is being able to translate those lessons into my day-to-day career as a DEI practitioner. Violence and all.

References

Adi, H. (2018). *Pan-Africanism: A history*. Bloomsbury.

Banton, C. A. (2019). *More auspicious shores: Barbadian migration to Liberia, Blackness, and the making of an African republic*. Cambridge University Press.

Barbados House of Assembly (BHA). (1818). *The report from a select committee of the House of Assembly, appointed to inquire into the origin, causes, and progress, of the late insurrection*. W. Williams, Mercury & Gazette.

Barrow, E. (1987). "No loitering on colonial premises": Address to the Barbados Constitutional Conference in London, July 1966. In Y. Haniff (Ed.), *Speeches by Errol Barrow*. Hansib Publications.

Beckles, H. M. (1998). Historicizing slavery in West Indian feminisms. *Feminist Review*, *59*(1), 34–56. https://doi.org/10.1080/014177898339442

Comissiong, D. (Ed.). (2021). *The Clement Payne story*. David Comissiong Publishing.

Denny, S. L. (2021). Edutocracy: A model of the new West Indian plantocracy in Barbados. *Sage Open*, *11*(2). https://doi.org/10.1177/21582440211030278

Espírito Santo, D. (2017). Possession consciousness, religious individualism, and subjectivity in Brazilian Umbanda. *Religion*, *47*(2), 179–202. https://doi.org/10.1080/0048721X.2016.1198839

Mathieu, S. J. (2010). *North of the color line: Migration and Black resistance in Canada, 1870–1955*. The University of North Carolina Press.

Moore, M. Z. (2022). Neo-colonialism in distance learning in Barbados and Canada. *Journal of Comparative & International Higher Education*, *14*(2), 152–165. https://doi.org/10.32674/jcihe.v14i2.3792

National Cultural Foundation (NCF). (2021). *Nineteen thirty-seven* (Resource guide). https://ncf.bb/2021/10/17/the-1937-riots-resource-kit/

Rockquemore, K. A., & Laszloffy, T. (2008). *The Black academic's guide to winning tenure—Without losing your soul*. Lynne Rienner Publishers.

Chapter 9

Emancipatory Violence

Introduction: Linking *Praxis*, History, and Emancipatory Violence

> If we put a bookmark in our MLK and instead dusted off The *Wretched of the Earth* by Frantz Fanon, we would, for one, be less dream-prone. For another, when pundits and presidential candidates speak of American values after an attack we would be reminded of the line: 'In the colonial context the colonist only quits undermining the colonized once the latter have proclaimed loud and clear that White values reign supreme. In the period of decolonization the colonized masses thumb their noses at these very values, shower them with insults and vomit them up. Such an occurrence normally goes unseen because, during decolonisation, certain colonized intellectuals have established a dialogue with the bourgeoisie of the colonizing country'. (Marshall, 2019, para. 9)

Emancipation, or to be emancipated, can be defined as 'to free from restraint, control, or the power of another especially: to free from bondage' (Merriam-Webster, n.d., para. 1). I like to approach myself and my work through a prism of contemplative pedagogies and the theoretical underpinnings of critical race theory and Black feminist thought and theory. So, let's think about what that actually means. *To be free*. To be free is to be emancipated, and to be emancipated is to be free. But what am I truly emancipated from? As a second-generation Black man, am I truly free from restraint at the hands of the justice system when my brothers and sisters are dodging bullets in the streets from those that look like me and those that are supposed to protect me? Am I free from the control of surveillance of Black bodies? Am I free from an unjust immigration system that continues to deny my existence in the Great White North? Am I free from the psychological and diachronic effects of Post-Traumatic Slave Syndrome? Am I free from the White supremacy that is embedded in the very fabric of my 'emancipation' and 'freedom'?

Unmasking DEI, 127–148

doi:10.1108/978-1-83708-356-520261009

Does DEI free me, and save me, from the omnipresent violence of living as a Black man in the Black Atlantic?

Chapter 8 reminded us that emancipation has always been contested and often forged through struggle. Chapter 9 pushes this conversation further by interrogating the concept of emancipatory violence as a radical reorientation of resistance. Drawing on Frantz Fanon, Nelson Mandela, and other revolutionaries, we explore how psychological, epistemic, and ideological disruption can serve as tools for liberation when assimilationist frameworks fail. This chapter asks: What does it mean to be truly free in a world where anti-Black violence persists in both overt and covert forms? This chapter does not advocate indiscriminate physical violence but rather redefines violence as a multidimensional response to structural oppression.

What Does It Mean to Be Free? Rethinking Emancipation

I want folks to let this sit with them: our history of enslavement, our history of colonialism, this country's ongoing history of settler colonialism, anti-Black racism, and White supremacy are defined through violence. This is something our society does not want to teach us, nor does it want us to know: our existence, and the *attempted erasure* of our existence, was a physically, psychologically, emotionally, and spiritually violent act. During the period of enslavement, we were dehumanized to justify our Christian God-given place as 'beasts of burden.' That is violence. We were beaten, maimed, and killed for profit. That is violence. We were legally stripped of our drums. Our language. Our beliefs. Displaced from our homes. That is violence. We are told we are not as 'smart' as the other children in class. That is violence. We are told to believe that our skin colour or hair isn't as 'pretty' as a cartoon character named Ariel. That is violence. So why do we consistently adopt a sanitized approach to Emancipation (DEI) and not acknowledge the violence that we experienced during the period of enslavement, the violence that we have yet to be truly emancipated from? Why do we continue to be told by a White supremacist system (that has no interest in our mental and psychological emancipation) to adopt the Santaclausification of Dr Martin Luther King, Jr. and not – as Dr Cornel West (2016) has termed – the approach of 'The Radical King'? Why do we not adopt the approach of Nanny Grigg, as she led the 1816 Easter Rebellion for freedom in Barbados? Or Amy Jacques Garvey, as she pushed our collective Black unity through Pan-Africanism? Why do we not adopt the approach of one of our greatest Black Pan-African thinkers, Frantz Fanon, and adopt his approach to freedom and emancipation through a theoretical understanding of violence?

Fanon and the Theory of Violence: Beyond Physical Confrontation

Some people reading this would argue that Fanon's (1963/2004) *The Wretched of the Earth*, particularly his chapter 'On Violence', is solely about the indiscriminate physical violence of murder of the colonist to effect change. He stated, 'for the last can be the first only after a murderous and decisive confrontation between the two protagonists. This determination...can only succeed by resorting to every means, including of course, violence' (Fanon, 1963/2004, p. 29). However, as it relates to our continued enslavement and the reparations of our emancipation, I approach this view on violence differently. If our enslaved and colonized kin were subjected to a variety of psychological, physical, and emotional terrorist violent warfare, we must first acknowledge said violence in order to learn to decolonize and emancipate ourselves through a collectively violent response. According to Fanon (1963/2004), 'Decolonization, therefore, implies the urgent need to thoroughly challenge the colonial situation' (p. 2).

The Violence of History: Enslavement, Colonialism, and Structural Oppression

We are still colonized beings in a settler colonial state. What I'm advocating for is not new, nor is it novel; however, the 21st century White supremacist discourse and the mechanisms of White violence, White fragility, and White guilt have curtailed our understanding of violence and how effective it has been, and will be, in our emancipation story. Fanon (1963/2004) has told us not to forget: 'The colonial regime owes its legitimacy to force and at no time does it ever endeavor to cover up this nature of things' (p. 42). Fanon (1963/2004) has told us not to forget: 'The colonized man liberates himself in and through violence' (p. 44). Fanon (1963/2004) has told us not to forget: 'Violence among the colonized will spread in proportion to the violence exerted by the colonial regime' (p. 46). We are in an environment where the oppressor has co-opted the language of the oppressed, manifesting their violence through the structures and institutions of White supremacy to continue to sanction our exclusion, marginalization, and death in all walks of life. What I want to make clear is that the violence I am advocating for is not in response to the physical violence of an occupying force, but to mitigate the effects of Post Traumatic Slave Syndrome, to mitigate the effects of the White supremacist institution of living and operating within a PWI, and to mitigate the effects of how we – as Black people – reconcile and navigate this nihilistic environment and the enslavement of our collective psychological Self.

One core challenge Black people face is living in an individualistic neoliberal environment that does not give us a chance to breathe. We are always searching for 'what's next?' In academia, it is about getting through comps, then writing your dissertation, then defending your dissertation, then finding the tenure track job, then getting research grants, publishing, getting tenure, and on, and on, and on. You can find yourself working for 20 years trying to get a permanent job. Killing your spirit and sense of Self along the way. We, and rightfully so, are so focused on this neoliberal understanding of our individual Self and our own socio-economic mobility as citizens. This has historically been a tool to divide and conquer our Black ancestors. We are then not given a chance to fully comprehend how we are, on a daily basis, in our offices and cubicles, breathing the recycled air of White supremacy. Where do we go from here? I understand the challenges. I understand that feeling of 'performance' and how we code switch in bureaucratic spaces to make those of a lighter hue more comfortable – not in the skin we are in, but the skin they are in. I understand the physical, emotional, spiritual, and psychological trauma this causes you. Every. Single. Day. I am not advocating for Black people to quit their jobs, but I am advocating for you to understand that what you are experiencing is a form of violence that is killing our collective spirit and productivity.

Psychological and Epistemic Violence: Post-Traumatic Slave Syndrome and Cultural Trauma

Reader, I want you to understand that these feelings are rooted in Post Traumatic Slave Syndrome (PTSS), a theory developed by Dr Joy DeGruy. DeGruy (2017) established that PTSS is a condition that 'exists when a population has experienced multigenerational trauma resulting from centuries of slavery and continues to experience oppression and institutionalized racism today' (p. 105). PTSS is reflected in feelings of hopelessness, depression, and a general self-destructive outlook; extreme feelings of suspicion and perceived negative motivations of others; violence against self, property, and others, including members of one's own group (friends, relatives, or acquaintances); and internalized racism. I also want you to understand that the system does not care about our mental health as it relates to racism. Why? Most people do not even know or think PTSS is a real and tangible condition that affects Black people across the Black Atlantic.

Black people are pathologized and blamed, or minimized, or forgotten; all patterns that have roots during our period of enslavement and its ominous, lingering cloud of White supremacy. Before we move forward, we must understand and acknowledge that 185 years later, we are not truly free from all the forms of violence that we were 'legally' emancipated from on 1 August 1834. But – and it is a big but – all is not lost. Black people in the Black Atlantic must understand how our cultural trauma is, according to Dr Michael J. Halloran (2019), 'defined as a state that occurs when a people's cultural worldview has been destabilized to the point where it does not effectively meet its . . . function of providing a buffer against basic anxiety and uncertainty' (p. 45).

We must confront these ideas head-on and demand change: How do I expand my cultural lens? How do I redefine 'violence' and dismantle the White violence woven into systems and institutions? This is not about checking boxes for diversity, equity, or inclusion; it is about reclaiming Négritude as resistance. It is about radical love, about honouring the brilliance and uniqueness of Blackness. Still, we must speak plainly about the anti-Black trauma that scars our ancestors and us.

Silence is complicity. Naming it is power.

Building on the Strengths of Our Ancestors

In practical terms, building on the strengths of our ancestors could be a simple reflection of our everyday interactions in the everyday; it could mean taking a pause on how taken-for-granted, daily actions perpetuate this anti-Black cultural trauma. For example, it might mean what I eat for lunch, what I wear to work, how I pronounce my words, whether I say people or persons, or if I am going to share what I really did for Caribana, Carnival, or Notting Hill. The age-old question becomes whether Black people in these spaces push for more. Does one push for more, knowing that there could, and would, be repercussions for pressing for one's humanity? In school, it may mean not getting a degree or being kicked out of school. In the workplace, it could mean getting fired and being unable to pay rent or keep your kids in daycare. In the streets, it may be the fine line between going to jail and losing your life. Do I change what is on the margins? Or do I continue to navigate a system without rocking the boat? The world is an anti-Black and violent space. I say that we respond with violence. We respond with a spiritual, psychological, and emotional violence that burns deep within our displaced Self. *A fire that is who we are.*

We channel the strength of those who came before us that fought back against the violence of enslavement and White supremacy, carving out a path to our true Emancipation: Frantz Fanon, Marcus Garvey, Marie-Joseph Angelique, Nanny Griggs, Chloe Cooley, and so many more. We respond against the violence that somehow our ancestors survived as they were marched from the interior to the coast, shackled and raped in the dungeons, abused and tortured on the ships, and worked to death in the Americas. There is a reason why the system does not want us to know about this violent history; if we knew, we would not be asking for change. We would be taking it.

Guerrilla Warfare as Metaphor: Rethinking Resistance Strategies

Captain Nelson J. Anderson, in his article 'Guerilla Warfare' from the April 1942 issue of Military Review, explains that the Spanish term 'guerrilla' literally translates to 'little war' (p. 42). Guerrilla warfare, also known as 'partisan warfare' or 'irregular warfare', refers to military activities conducted by small, independent units in an irregular manner, often without formal military organization, in conjunction with a regular war.

Engaging in concepts of guerrilla warfare may seem to be a drastic measure for finding new concepts to confront anti-Black racism. To be clear, this chapter uses guerrilla warfare as a metaphor for adaptive, decentralized resistance strategies, not as a call for physical violence. However, I, and many before me, have established that anti-Black racism is violent; it is the literal and figurative Black death by weathering, death by neglect, and overt and covert death by the hands of the state. If we do not engage with this understanding of epistemic violence – the (un)learning of the truth of systemic dehumanization and discarding of Black histories, realities, and bodies – and of the physical and psychological violence against Black people, we will continue to try to adopt assimilationist policies of DEI, thinking that this will fix the problem. The state has declared war against Black people, and the only way to fight back is to adopt and adapt real-world historical examples of tactics that overthrew oppressive regimes. This concept is crucial to understand and relate to Shadow Strategies, emphasizing that our response involves violence through guerrilla warfare (Black-first *praxis*) rather than traditional means (DEI).

So what is guerrilla warfare? Anderson, in 1942, noted that guerrilla warfare has been a component of both major and minor wars throughout history and is mentioned in many historical accounts of past and present conflicts. Regarding tactics, Anderson (1942) highlighted that while guerrilla and orthodox warfare can be effectively combined, their tactics differ significantly. Orthodox operations involve constant activity and movement, whereas guerrilla warfare focuses on sudden strikes followed by retreat. Unlike regular warfare, guerrilla tactics do not include transforming a moving situation into a defensive position or engaging in decisive battles. Instead, guerrilla warfare avoids fixed passive defences common in orthodox war. A 'win' does not mean a 'win' in a traditional sense.

Think about it in this way: through traditional DEI measures, one goal or focus, typically, is to get more Black people in positions of leadership. It is mainly focused on increasing representation, or the 'I' of including more Black skins/White masks into positions of leadership. These leaders are then assigned to carry out the same oppressive culture that they managed to 'overcome' to get where they were. That is a traditional DEI win; a win that is defined as the ability to gain territory (or boardroom space) of traditional warfare. However, what if we redefined a 'win'? That the ultimate goal was not to get into a boardroom (which, yes, would ultimately happen under a complete overthrow of the Oppressor, the power-*full*), but what if a 'win' was an ideal that the warring side did not know what hit them? What if the ultimate win wasn't just a Black CEO, or Black Prime Minister, or Black President, but the emancipation and liberation of our collective Selves to reach our humanity? What if the first step was to clearly articulate our 'wins'?

Although guerrilla warfare has not been the primary method for resolving major military conflicts, it has significantly influenced the outcomes of many wars. Black-first approaches to change may not be the sole method for change. When it comes to the needless violence of modern warfare, war is fought on unlimited possibilities and can be conducted on land, in the air, in the water, and soon enough, in space. Again, we need to use these models of warfare, albeit difficult for many to comprehend and accept, to understand that one single approach to change – DEI – will not work. Having the world's greatest army is not going to help in a war at sea. DEI is fighting a naval battle with a cruise ship. If we are not engaging and understanding the multiple fields of battle, we will meet our Waterloo 10 times out of 10. However, if we know we are a lesser resourced contingent, that we already exist in the metropole, that we have tools to 'be included,' we can try to capitalize on our ability to embody multiple identities and consciousness; to code switch and code mesh and infiltrate systems as our comrades fight the good fight from places unknown. In the context of the Japanese invasion of China in the 1930s and 1940s, guerrilla warfare, combined with traditional warfare, allowed the poorly equipped and partly trained Chinese forces to hold off the well-equipped and highly trained Japanese for about five years. Despite Japanese expectations that the Chinese population in occupied areas would support them, the Japanese could only control territory within rifle range of military garrisons and guarded supply routes. We can take other examples of the Vietnam War, the multiple wars in Afghanistan, the continued resistance of Indigenous peoples against settler colonialism in Canada, anti-colonial movements across the African Continent, and, I would say, quoting Rinaldo Walcott (2021), the long emancipation of Black peoples. If we turn our minds to the history books, examples of struggles and uprisings against systems, and adapt that ethos of freedom and liberation, we can see that DEI is not the antidote to anti-Black racism.

Revisiting (Some) Black Revolutionaries: Mandela, King, and the Politics of Struggle

> The oppressor must be liberated just as surely as the oppressed.
> Nelson Mandela (1995, p. 624)

Santaclausification and the Sanitizing of Radical Histories

Santaclausification. A funny term, with very misleading implications. A way to rewrite the truth, to make it palatable for all. Santa Claus, for many children and adults, is a jovial character who brings no harm. He spreads love and cheer for billions across the globe. He brings joy in times of crisis, poverty, and famine. He even stops wars in their tracks (for a day, at least). Now, reimagine DEI and Black revolutionaries through the framework of Santaclausification: the fire, the passion, the violence that brought (and brought down) names such as Nelson Mandela and Dr Martin Luther King Jr. have now become beacons for tolerance and 'inclusion' while wiping away the true path. The history books casually omit the fact that a White man assassinated Dr King Jr. We casually omit the fact that Dr King Jr. warned us of (White) DEI practitioners as he wrote from a Birmingham jail in 1963:

> I have almost reached the regrettable conclusion that the Negro's great stumbling block in his stride toward freedom is not the White Citizen's Counciler or the Ku Klux Klanner, but the White moderate, who is more devoted to 'order' than to justice; who prefers a negative peace which is the absence of tension to a positive peace which is the presence of justice; who constantly

> says: 'I agree with you in the goal you seek, but I cannot agree with your methods of direct action'. (para. 19)

Do the most vocal defenders of DEI not take this approach of appeasement? Of working within the system, but not changing said system, to ostensibly achieve similar goals of 'diversity' within (in)equitable systems? The White moderate, the progressive liberal, and the 'well-meaning' educator all speak of change, but adopt and reinforce systems that perpetuate assimilation and integration of Du Bois' (1903) invocation of the *talented tenth*, or the 'right kind of Black' that will preach the gospel of DEI and its many exclusionary practices, while saying, 'Well, it worked for me, so it should work for you'. We see this in the rhetoric surrounding the *model minority* – the individual(s) who went above and beyond to internalize the psychological violence of an anti-Black society and achieved against seemingly insurmountable odds. Moreover, we see this, particularly in North America, among 'racial groups' such as East Asians. Black people can achieve, insofar as they are in accepted 'racialized' spaces (such as entertainment or athletics) or of 'exceptional merit.'

The Misplaced Ideals of 'Black Excellence': 'Exceptional Merit' and the Roots of Black Exceptionalism

This idea of having to work 'twice as hard' to achieve 'half as much' is not anecdotal. In Canada, the process of being an 'exception' was written in its racist early-to-mid 20th-century immigration laws. The Acting Deputy Minister of the Immigration Branch, C. E. S. Smith wrote to the Director, Laval Fortier, 10 March 1958, that 'it has been our long standing practice to deal favourably with British subjects of White race from the British West Indies', and not encourage emigrants outside of the class of domestics, 'graduate nurses, qualified stenographers, etc' (as cited in Satzewich, 1991, p. 126). However, he admitted:

> We are continually being accused of discrimination against the coloured race in this area and our rebuttal has been that there is no racial discrimination and that only persons accepted are those clearly defined in the admissible class and those with exceptional merit. (Smith, 1958, as cited in Satzewich, 1991, p. 126, author's emphasis)

These arbitrary selection criteria created cases of emigrants of *exceptional merit* – those above and beyond the criteria needed for entry of White emigrants – and facilitated the continued exclusion of whomever Canadian immigration officials simply did not like by virtue of being the Other. Most importantly, racism was hidden under ostensibly reasonable, but still illogical, means for exclusion. This included climate discrimination that many Barbadians faced once applying to emigrate to Canada, who received the response that they would not be able to 'weather' the cold and harsh Canadian climate. If they still managed to jump through all of these hoops, they were of *exceptional merit*. I write this to say that this idea of DEI draws from this rhetoric of exceptionalism (i.e. the tokenism and 'only ones'), but also the presence of international Black revolutionaries that managed to exceed the expectations of White society. However, it created, with lasting effects to this day, a challenge where the 'bad side' of these revolutionaries is erased as they are Santaclausified (i.e. White-washed). Black people are then forced to believe that the DEI philosophy of 'inclusion' and 'representation' is how long-standing human rights, civil rights, and liberation movements were achieved by notable figures such as Dr King Jr. and Nelson Mandela. Meanwhile, it was really through bloodshed, death, self-sacrifice, and incarceration.

Nelson Mandela and Dr King Jr.: The Politics of Violence and Change-Making in a World of Appeasement

Nelson Mandela is often a name that is (mis)used in DEI parlance of 'turn the other cheek' and love thy neighbour. His history, and that of South Africa, was painted at the turn of the millennium as the bastion of diversity, equity, and inclusivity. In reality, and in broad strokes, this was not the full truth, and the legacies of apartheid continue to destabilize and cause fissures within the country. However, the question here is not necessarily about South Africa in its present state, but how major aspects of Nelson Mandela, a true Black revolutionary, were Santaclausified to fit neat narratives of diversity, equity, and inclusion; stories that do not, and will not, challenge the status quo.

From his autobiography, *Long Walk to Freedom: The Autobiography of Nelson Mandela*, Nelson Mandela (1995) gave keen insight into how he was able to navigate, challenge, and ultimately disrupt the White supremacist apartheid system. Nelson Mandela's education played a crucial role in shaping his worldview and strategies. As a young man in Johannesburg in the early 1940s who completed his BA by the end of 1942, he noted:

> I moved in circles where common sense and practical experience were more important than high academic qualifications. Even as I was receiving my degree, I realized that hardly anything I had learned at university seemed relevant in my new environment. (Mandela, 1995, p. 89)

Further, Mandela (1995) believed that:

> Education is the great engine of personal development. It is through education that the daughter of a peasant can become a doctor, that the son of a mineworker can become the head of the mine, that the child of farmworkers can become the president of a great nation. It is what we make out of what we have, not what we are given, that separates one person from another. (p. 166)

During the early to mid-20th century, South Africa's education system was deeply racist, with the government spending six times more on educating White students compared to African students. Education for Africans was not compulsory and was only free at the primary level. As a result, fewer than half of African children of school age attended school, and only a tiny number graduated from secondary school. The 1953 *Bantu Education Act* marked a significant shift in South African education, as the Afrikaner nationalist government took control of African education, previously dominated by foreign churches and missionaries (Mandela, 1995). Schools that did not transfer control to the government would lose subsidies, effectively resulting in 'no education for Africans' (Mandela, 1995). Dr Hendrik Verwoerd, the Minister of Bantu education, stated that education 'must train and teach people in accordance with their opportunities in life', asserting that 'there is no place for the Bantu in the European community above the level of certain forms of labor' (Mandela, 1995, p. 167). According to Mandela (1995), this policy led to the emergence of the angriest, most rebellious generation of Black youth in the 1970s. Mandela's reflection on the impact of the *Bantu Education Act*, which produced a generation of rebellious Black youth, highlights the long-term consequences of systemic inequities.

Mandela studied law at the University of Fort Hare and later at the University of Witwatersrand, which equipped him with the knowledge to understand and navigate the legal system. His training and accreditation as a lawyer gave him the tools to understand, navigate, and ultimately dismantle White supremacist systems. Mandela (1995) used the law as a means for change, understanding both legal and revolutionary systems. He believed in leveraging the legal framework to challenge apartheid and promote justice (Mandela, 1995). His law degree and legal training were akin to the DEI notion of 'inclusion' within an inequitable system. Mandela was a key figure in the African National Congress (ANC), which was instrumental in mobilizing collective groups and individuals against apartheid. The ANC's efforts were rooted in traditional African values, while also confronting colonial and White supremacist systems. His approach involved working with various people systems. He valued personal connections and mentorship, believed in the power of collective action and unity, respected and incorporated traditional African values and practices, fought against the remnants of colonial oppression, actively opposed and sought to dismantle the White supremacist structures in South Africa, garnered international support and aid to bolster the anti-apartheid movement, and promoted Pan-African solidarity and cooperation (Mandela, 1995). Mandela's time in prison was a testament to his resilience and strategic thinking, as he used his imprisonment to strengthen his resolve and plan for the future.

Mandela navigated various political systems, adapting his tactics as needed. He was known for his patience, listening skills, and collaboration, while remaining steadfast to his principles. Mandela was pragmatic in his approach, sometimes resorting to violence when peaceful means were ineffective. However, he always prioritized dialogue and negotiation. His patience and ability to listen to others were key to his leadership. He valued diverse perspectives and sought consensus. Mandela collaborated with others but remained unwavering in his principles. He stood up for others and spoke on their behalf, embodying the spirit of a true leader. Mandela's family ties were important to him, providing emotional support and grounding him throughout his struggles. Mandela's foresight and strategic thinking were evident in his long-term vision for a democratic South Africa. He planned meticulously and adapted his strategies to changing circumstances (Mandela, 1995).

These insights from Mandela's life and work provide a rich context for historicizing the pros and cons of DEI. Mandela's insights into the apartheid education system highlight the systemic inequalities that marginalized African students and the critical need for systemic changes; changes that in the 2020s may be referred to as DEI, critical race, Black Studies, or 'woke' education. However, the Apartheid government's disproportionate spending on White students and the lack of compulsory education for Black Africans created significant barriers to educational attainment and personal development for the majority of the population. Mandela's belief in education as a powerful tool for personal development underscores the importance of equitable access to education in fostering diversity and inclusion. His statement that education allows individuals from disadvantaged backgrounds to achieve great things emphasizes the need for inclusive educational policies that provide equal opportunities for all, regardless of their socio-economic status or racial background. Some would argue, particularly around his positioning of 'inclusion' and being against the Black Consciousness Movement, that we aligned closer to the DEI mantra of 'inclusion for all.' Mandela did not approve of an exclusionary movement that did not involve Whites. He stated that BCM:

> was less a movement than a philosophy and grew out of the idea that [B]lacks must first liberate themselves from the sense of psychological inferiority bred by three centuries of White rule. Only then could the people rise up in confidence and truly liberate themselves from repression. (Mandela, 1995, p. 486)

My Deep and Conflicted Reflections on Robben Island

I will admit, when I travelled to Robben Island in 2023 in my role as Associate Vice-President, Equity, Diversity, Inclusion, and Anti-Racism, I did not have the same feeling of 'inclusion' and turning the other cheek. As an historian, it is very important for me to 'feel' history, to walk in spaces that I have read in books or archives, to feel the same sun that an enslaved ancestor felt hundreds of years ago, or to sit in the same cell as Mandela. As I walked those steps through the prison yard and other buildings (as you are not allowed to go in his cell), I did not have a feeling of anger, but one of incredulity. I could understand, but not necessarily agree with, how one person (and many others before and after him) could be Santaclausified as the harbinger of hope, of diversity, and of inclusion by the very same people that dehumanized and caged him as an animal for nearly three decades. It is a travesty that while the DEI proponents advocate for the non-confrontational appeasement approach to changing systems, and like many of whom who point to the likes of Mandela, omit key aspects of his pre-imprisoned life. This is the individual that was educated, knew the law, knew the system, and one who had always advocated for non-violent approaches to change, but also knew that violence was the only language the Oppressor understood. Yes, many have and will rightfully argue that this approach was self-defence, as per the 1960s approach of the Black Panther Party for Self-Defence. And yes, if indiscriminate violence is enacted on someone, it is their right to self-defence. The challenge that is faced in the 2020s is that the general population do not understand the shape-shifting forms of violence; they do not understand forms of violence that are not as egregious, as explicit, as *recorded* as the 8 minutes and 46 seconds.

The Big Issue of 'Micro-Aggressions': When DEI Doesn't Solve the Real Pain We Experience

> The 'steady accumulation of a thousand slights?' (Mandela, 1995 p. 95)

In sports, it is often said that referees tend to penalize the player who retaliates rather than the one who initiated the aggression. While cameras, other players, and fans may witness the initial act, the player who responds is usually the one who gets caught and penalized, thus being perceived as the aggressor. This adage highlights a common issue in sports officiating where the focus is on the visible act of retaliation rather than the unseen provocation. It underscores the challenges referees face in making fair judgments, as they may not always witness the initial act of aggression. This situation can lead to a sense of injustice for the player who was defending themselves, as they are punished while the true aggressor goes unpenalized. The broader implication of this scenario can be related to various aspects of life and justice systems, where reactions are often more visible and scrutinized than the actions that provoke them. It emphasizes the importance of context and the need for comprehensive observation and understanding before making judgments. This principle can be applied to ensure fairness and equity in both sports and broader societal contexts. But more importantly, it can and does relegate 'change' to 'peaceful' approaches such as DEI, approaches that do not openly confront systemic oppressive violence, whether it be physical, psychological and emotional. The challenge we face is this: How does one make change when the violence they face is not egregious or a 'spectacle' like the 8 minutes and 46 seconds? When the violence does not in fact *look* violent? What do we do with these day-to-day mosquito bites?

In DEI parlance, we refer to these '1000 slights' as micro-aggressions or micro-inequities. I like to refer to them as macro-aggressions as these 'slights' are deliberate and debilitating. Having someone(s) ask you where you are from or if they can touch your hair on a daily basis will produce an anger and a rebelliousness to fight against the system, as Mandela (1995) identified. That being said, it can also, and most often does, produce self-hate, despair, and a complete rejection of one's physical and cultural Blackness. Calvin L. Warren (2015) and other scholars refer to this as *Black nihilism*; a sense of pessimism among Black people for improving their life conditions under the ominous cloak of intertwining forms of anti-Black racism. Without hope, what is one to do? However, there is the possibility to channel this despair through the (re)visiting of Black figures such as Mandela. One area, similar to that of Dr King Jr. and others, is to understand the relationship of race and class, as Mandela (1995) believed, 'I found myself strongly drawn to a classless society, which, to my mind was similar to traditional African culture where life was shared and communal' (p. 120). It is also to understand that the resistance to change falls in the understanding and belief that the White majority fears DEI as they will no longer be in the majority, nor have absolute or hegemonic power and control over non-White bodies. Mandela (1995) stated, 'The White man fears democracy because he will no longer be in the majority' (p. 368). What we have learnt from Mandela is that power does not give up power for the sake of it, and we can argue that a democratic process is much like DEI – following a system that on the surface is benevolent and fair for all, but creates boundaries and barriers to achieving true equity and subsequently equality. Change requires struggle, and as Mandela (1995) wrote, 'The idea that history progresses through struggle and change occurs in revolutionary jumps was similarly appealing' (p. 120).

A Different View of Mandela's Legacy

Here is where the conversation on Mandela shifts and the santaclausification begins. Yes, Mandela (1995) called for non-violent protests and wrote, 'I called for nonviolent protest for as long as it was effective' (p. 128). In 1961, after he was acquitted in the 1950s Treason Trial, he referred to the 'Old African expression … *Sebatana ha se bokwe ka diatla* (The attacks of the wild beast cannot be averted with only bare hands)' (p. 271). The apartheid state 'had given us no alternative to violence… it was wrong and immoral to subject our people to armed attacks by the state without offering them some kind of alternative' (Mandela, 1995, p. 272).

Umkhonto we Sizwe (MK), the military organization led by Nelson Mandela, was mandated to 'wage acts of violence against the state' with the intention to start with actions 'least violent to individuals but most damaging to the state' (Mandela, 1995, p. 274). He studied South African history to understand how to initiate a revolution and considered four types of violent activities: sabotage, guerrilla warfare, terrorism, and open revolution. Mandela (1995) chose sabotage because 'it did not involve loss of life [so] it offered the best hope for reconciliation among the races afterward' (p. 285). Its manifesto stated:

> The time comes in life of any nation when there remain only two choices: submit or fight. That time has now come to South Africa. We shall not submit and we have no choice but to hit back by all means within our power in defence of our people, our future and our freedom. (Mandela, 1995, p. 285)

Mandela's involvement in sabotage led to his long imprisonment in July 1963. During his trial, he argued that sabotage was the 'best hope for future race relations', as:

> we felt it our duty to make preparations as a long-term undertaking to use force in order to defend ourselves against force. If war were inevitable, we wanted the fight to be conducted on terms most favourable to our people. The fight which held out prospects best for us and the least risk of life to both sides was guerrilla warfare. (Mandela, 1995, p. 365)

Mandela (1995) acknowledged the tragic accidents involving civilian deaths during car bombings in the 1980s, stating, 'The killing of civilians was a tragic accident, and I felt a profound horror at the death toll...I knew that such accidents were the inevitable consequence of the decision to embark on a military struggle' (p. 518). He emphasized that the armed struggle was imposed by the apartheid regime's violence.

In January 1985, Mandela was offered freedom if he 'unconditionally rejected violence as a political instrument' (Mandela, 1995, p. 521). He responded, 'I am not a violent man...It was only then, when all other forms of resistance were no longer open to us, that we turned to armed struggle' (Mandela, 1995, pp. 522–523). He called on Botha to renounce violence and dismantle apartheid.

Mandela viewed violence as a means to an end, necessary to initiate negotiations after over 20 years of armed struggle. He warned, 'If we did not start a dialogue soon, both sides would be plunged into a dark night of oppression, violence, and war' (Mandela, 1995, p. 525). While he was not willing to renounce violence, he affirmed that 'violence could never be the ultimate solution to the situation in South Africa' and that a negotiated understanding was essential (Mandela, 1995, p. 528). He stated, 'it is always the oppressor, not the oppressed, who dictates the form of the struggle. If the oppressor uses violence, the oppressed have no alternative but to respond violently' (Mandela, 1995, p. 537). Even after Mandela's release in early 1990, the armed struggle continued, and state-sanctioned violence persisted in destabilizing the country.

Re-Orienting Our Views on Violence: Unapologetic Black Bodies in White Spaces

How can we argue that violence was not a fundamental feature of Mandela's revolutionary insight to end apartheid? Why can't we admit that this feature of 'violence' is omitted from the 'clean,' santaclausified narrative of a palatable DEI figure? Writers, such as Tom Lodge (2006) in *Mandela: A Critical Life*, described a less confrontational figure. Humans are complex beings; however, it is crucially important that the world understands the fullness of one's character and points of view. It is argued, particularly in DEI circles, that Malcolm X was simply an anti-White demagogue. Meanwhile, Dr King Jr. was the standard-bearer for tolerance and acceptance of White people, which is quite interesting but does not capture the fullness of Dr King Jr. In his 1959 essay, 'The Social Organization of Non-Violence', Dr King Jr. describes his three different views on violence. Firstly, is his commonly known approach of 'pure nonviolence', which he argues 'cannot readily or easily attract large masses, for it requires extraordinary discipline and courage' (King, 1959, p. 5). Secondly, self-defence, 'which all societies from the most primitive to the most cultured and civilized, accept as moral and legal' (King, 1959, p. 6). Thirdly is the 'advocacy of violence as a tool of advancement, organized as in warfare, deliberately and consciously' (King, 1959, p. 6).

While Dr King Jr. does not openly support this 'advocacy of violence', I see this as a play on words on violence and its many forms. He argues that by initiating violence, Negroes can provoke 'questions about the necessity for it, and inevitably is blamed for its consequences'; however, when the 'Negro uses force in self-defense he does not forfeit support – he may even win it, by the courage and self-respect it reflects' (King, 1959, p. 6). If one is being subject to historical and contemporary violence, any reaction should, and must, be deemed as a form of self-defence. That being said, our contemporary society is not framed, nor understood in the mainstream as a violent state. This is what Gayatri Chakravorty Spivak (1988) described as the violence that occurs when the knowledge and experiences of less powerful groups are ignored or dismissed by those in power. This can happen when certain types of knowledge are seen as more valuable than others, leading to the silencing of marginalized voices. Producing knowledge, particularly within a PWI, that does not 'fit' specific traditional disciplines (such as Black-first *praxis*) is a form of (self-defensive) violence.

Along with the way I dress on campus and present as a senior executive, I practice this form of violence daily. If we re-orient our views on violence, and accept the reality of epistemic violence, we can see that the ethos of a violent uprising against the status quo is a valid means of moving forward. I draw from the teachings of the supposed opposites of Dr King Jr. and Malcolm X.

The conversation never rests with the understanding that, nearing the ends of their lives, Dr King Jr. and Malcolm X evolved and began to share many of the same perspectives on how to liberate Black people. Dr King Jr. began to adopt more of an 'action-oriented' position as opposed to the passive incrementalism that the Santaclausified historiography of his work has created. This leads to perspectives from Lodge (2006) and other scholars that, while true, do not capture the fullness of Mandela and the fullness of systemic anti-Black racism. Lodge (2006) wrote that Mandela's 'moral standing as a leader was enormously enhanced by his imprisonment' and how he followed order and procedure in prison, which helped 'preserve his commitment to orderly political process, a commitment that contrasted sharply with the more apocalyptic perceptions of many of his contemporaries during the 1970s and 1980s' (p. 10). This is essentially the description of the 'I' in DEI; to be included, and 'morally' accepted, one must conform and assimilate to the dominate ways of being. Even though Mandela himself described that he was not a violent person, the South African apartheid state was violent and set the terms of engagement; as Mandela wrote, the state would only respond and listen to a language they spoke, violence. Lodge (2006) argued that Mandela was shaped by:

> a politics of grace and honour that, notwithstanding its conservatism, was probably the only politics that could have enabled South Africa's relatively peaceful transition to democracy, a transition that more than a decade later appears to have resulted in a stable constitutional order. (p. 12)

I am not arguing that he did not aim to 'defeat one's opponents without humiliation' (Mandela, 1995, p. xii); however, the minimization of violence at the hands of the state, before, during, and after Mandela's imprisonment, does not accurately portray how violent civil disobedience – in self-defence against a violent oppressive state – was the catalyst for change in South Africa. The folklore of peace as the catalyst for change omits thousands of years of human history where violence undergirded most social movements. White women needed anti-Black enslavement for first-wave feminism; the post-war human rights and decolonization movements needed the Second World War; Dr King Jr. lived under the backdrop of the Cold War and its hot wars across the globe; and appeasement DEI in 2020 needed the 8 minutes and 46 seconds of Black Death.

Fred Hampton and Revolutionary *Praxis*: Lessons for Today

> Politics is war without bloodshed, and war is politics with bloodshed. (Hampton, 1969, p. 6)

> We in the Black Panther Party...went into the valley knowing that the people are in the valley, knowing that our enemies are on the mountain. (Hampton, 1969, p. 10)

> And we've got to go up on the mountain top not for the purpose of living his life style and living like he lives. We've got to go up on the mountain top to make this motherfucker understand, goddamnit, that we are coming from the valley! (Hampton, 1969, p. 6)

Fred Hampton, Deputy Chairman of the Black Panther Party, delivered his 'Power Anywhere Where There's People' speech in 1969, the year of his untimely murder at the age of 21. As it came to revolution (which I argue should and could be the ultimate goal of DEI alongside liberation), Hampton (1969) stated:

> A lot of people get the word 'revolution' mixed up and they think revolution's a bad word. Revolution is nothing but like having a sore on your body, and then you put something on that sore to cure that infection. And I'm telling you that we're living in an infectious society right now. I'm telling you that we're living in in a sick society. ... And anybody that endorses integrating into this sick society before it's cleaned up is a man who's committing a crime against the people. (p. 2)

Fred Hampton's quote addresses the common misconception that revolution is inherently negative, arguing instead that it is a necessary process for healing. He uses the metaphor of a sore or infection to describe society, suggesting that just as a sore needs treatment to heal, society requires revolutionary change to address its deep-rooted issues. Hampton describes the current state of society as 'infectious' and 'sick', implying that it is plagued by systemic problems that need to be addressed. He, as I do, criticizes the idea of integrating into a flawed system without first addressing its problems, asserting that doing so is akin to endorsing and perpetuating the existing issues, which he views as a crime against the people. DEI, or including Black skin with White masks into an inequitable system, can and does cause more harm. DEI does not address the root systemic causes of anti-Black racism, nor does it challenge the fundamental inequities embedded in systems ostensibly based on 'merit' or 'excellence.' It simply asks Black bodies to adopt neo-colonial modes of life. DEI is not revolutionary, but, as I have mentioned, serves as a form of appeasement to the wills of the dominant minority. Akin to the language in academic circles of 'publish or die,' the ethos of DEI is 'conform or stay out.' Overall, Hampton (1969) emphasizes the necessity of revolution as a means to heal and improve society, rather than simply accepting and integrating into its flawed state. His words reflect a deep commitment to social justice and systemic change. As Hampton (1969) stated, 'revolution is change' (p. 4).

We also must go back to the historical examples of revolution that can, and should, drive our Black-first *praxis*. C. L. R. James (1963), in his book *The Black Jacobins: Toussaint L'Ouverture and the San Domingo Revolution*, discusses the deep-rooted racial distinctions, their impact on society, and revolutionary change. He notes that for many, the difference between a White person and a person of colour was fundamental and worth defending at all costs. James (1963) also addresses the tendency of some to downplay the horrors of enslavement to foster national pride or ease a troubled conscience. Through his seminal work on the San Domingo (Haitian) Revolution, James (1963) describes various forms of resistance among enslaved people, including suicide as a way to spite their owners and their role as a 'modern proletariat' who learnt that isolated efforts were futile. Voodoo played a significant role in their communication and planning, with enslaved people travelling miles to participate in rituals and discuss political news. This is a form of violence against the Christian religious doctrine. Boukman, a high priest, led the charge, urging enslaved people to reject the god of the Whites and listen to the voice of liberty.

In every revolution, decisive action is crucial, as hesitation can lead to failure (James, 1963). Toussaint L'Ouverture initially kept his master's enslaved people in order, but eventually joined the revolted enslaved peoples, recognizing his destiny as their leader. He trained a few hundred devoted men, organizing them into an army capable of fighting European troops through well-planned attacks based on numerical superiority. James (1963) emphasizes the importance of the masses as the foundation of Toussaint's power, which grew with his influence over them. Political power was seen as a means to an end, with the restoration of agriculture being crucial for San Domingo's salvation. Strategic alliances were essential, with Toussaint leveraging offers from Spaniards for guns and ammunition while still advocating for freedom for Blacks (James, 1963).

What we also must learn is that failures in leadership often result in shattering blows to the masses, not from enemy bullets but from their own leaders' indecision. The Negro Code of 1685 authorized marriage between Whites and enslaved peoples, granting freedom to the woman and her children, but as the population grew, Whites discarded this convention (James, 1963). What was described as 'Mulattoes', despite amassing wealth, were treated as second-class citizens and often supported the royalist bureaucracy and military. Maintaining White structures and industriousness was seen as the ultimate guarantee of freedom, with Toussaint emphasizing personal industry, social morality, and racial equality, authorizing the Slave Trade in the Constitution and ensuring that Africans would be free upon arrival (James, 1963).

What we must remember, in our 2020 parlance and relationship with appeasement DEI and the Negro-Apocalypse, is that moderation or capitulation during a revolution can be detrimental, as seen in Toussaint's reluctance to fight during the war of independence, which ultimately led to destruction. Dessalines, on the other hand, advocated for violent means to achieve independence, massacring Whites to strike terror into French detachments. James (1963) concludes, as is key in this chapter and the ethos of this book, that the first step to freedom is to embrace Black or African identity, as clearing the stigma of inferiority was essential for liberation.

Ideological Suicide and Everyday Resistance: From Enslavement to Modern Workplaces

> The negroes are so willful and loth to leave their own country, that they have often leap'd out of the canoes, boat and ship, into the sea, and kept under water till they were drowned, to avoid being taken up and saved by our boats, which pursued them; they

> having a more dreadful apprehension of Barbadoes (sic) than we can have of hell.
>
> Hannibal, Captain of the English Slave Ship, (1694, as cited in Beckles, 2013, p. 47)
>
> Suicide as an act of resistance remained commonplace.
>
> Hilary Beckles (2013, p. 48)

This may be jarring to some, but suicide and infanticide were common acts of resistance for Black people during the period of enslavement and the Transatlantic Slave Trade. We typically do not think of death, particularly at the hands of one's own self, as a form of resistance. Yes, we understand martyrdom, and some can empathize with its virtues. But imagine being from a place – Barbados – that your ancestors would rather kill themselves than get shipped to. Imagine how the place of your parents' birth was the living reality of hell, not just an ominous place spread through religious doctrine. This reality hit me when I first visited the Cape Coast Castle, or what I refer to as the Factory of Death, in Ghana. As the tour guide took us down into the 'male slave dungeon,' I slipped. It did not seem like a big deal at the time. However, they then explained to us that the room we were in, where we were all sweating profusely and having difficulty breathing, was where men spent six to eight weeks packed like sardines. These men were waiting to be packed, again, like sardines on ships for six to eight weeks, crossing the Atlantic on their way to hell. The guide then told us about the floors; that these floors we were standing on were all original from the time of enslavement and the Trade. He explained how the enslavers would pack hay over the blood, bodies, and faeces. Over time, this mix of my Black kin became fabrics of the hell they waited to be shipped to.

For me, the ground was not nearly as terrifying as the roof. Still sweating, the guide told us to look up at the largest hole in the room. What the enslavers had done was build a church right on top of the dungeon. The purpose was two-fold. Firstly, it was to show my enslaved kin that salvation was above (in heaven) and through a (White) God. Secondly, it was to strike fear in the (White) churchgoers that the real hell was just one level below them. It is a terrifying idea to think that real people experienced the trauma that drives our contemporary nightmares; nightmares that strike fear in our lives and drive conformity and obedience. Imagine that it was my kin, my ancestors, my blood, and people like me that sat in those spaces, on their way to the second level of hell that was Barbados. It was in that moment that I could understand and even empathize with the ideas of suicide and infanticide as forms of resistance, revolution, and liberation.

Frantz Fanon (1963/2004) in *The Wretched of the Earth*, viewed suicide not merely as an act of despair but as a form of resistance against colonial oppression. He recognized that for some individuals, taking their own life could be a way to reclaim autonomy and protest against the dehumanizing conditions imposed by colonial powers. This perspective aligns with his broader views on the necessity of violent resistance to achieve decolonization (Fanon, 1963/2004).

C. L. R. James (1963) wrote that during enslavement, 'Suicide was a common habit [of slaves] . . . to spite their owner' (p. 15). If you think about it, the idea is horrifying, but quite simple; if your body is labour, and labour is profit, remove your body, and people lose profit. I am not advocating for death; however, through a Black-first *praxis*, and learning from the liberation, resistance, and revolutionary movements of our past, we need to take close, and often times uncomfortable, looks at the actions of our ancestors. We need to be mindful that self-immolation was, and is, a function of liberation. If we look broadly at the definition of suicide in terms of removing one's body, labour, and Self from being exploited for the gain of others, it may mean that 'career suicide' is quitting a job, doing the bare minimum, or refusing to conform to particular office norms that may cost you a raise or a promotion.

Contemporary Examples: Shadow Strategies and Career Resistance

These office norms may cost you your personal livelihood; however, it has the potential to force the oppressor to find avenues to appease and/or manipulate others to work. For instance, it reinforces the neoliberal sentiment of meritocracy and 'keeping up with the Joneses,' or an environment promoting the idea that everyone wants to move up and be the 'boss' or the 'leader' and rise up the ranks. If not, you are not succeeding in your career and should be shunned for that. It aligns with the ideal of DEI programmes that reinforce 'sponsorship' or 'mentorship,' and 'leadership programmes' that promote the idea that the only way for one to be 'successful' in one's career is to always 'move up.' While this may be the case for some, we must take a step back and truly understand what the point of a career is. What is the point of a career in academia or in the public service? Is it always striving for more, about moving up the ladder, about being a C-suiter? Is that the point, or what we have been conditioned to believe is the point? The mantra of DEI simply reinforces that to be 'successful' is to have more Black faces put on White masks. Why must Black people ascribe to this notion? Yes, to be successful during the slave trade, was to remove one's labour and die. This ideal should be taken seriously. What I mean to say here is that we should take lessons from our ancestors, ones that created the paths, options, and ultimately threats to the Traders and plantocracy; that we as Black people are willing to give up our existence before our spirits are dehumanized and our bodies are exploited. The challenge we face in the 2020s is fully articulating what this means in the workplace.

The question remains, why do we – Black people – settle for the crumbs of advancements in DEI in PWIs, when the PWI will never be the space that will allow us to reach our full liberation and actualization as human beings? I think that the issue comes down to the fact that, despite historical evidence of the contrary (e.g. Black and non-White men fighting in the World Wars believing that it would 'prove' their masculinity and 'worth' to White colonizers as 'loyal subjects'), trying to 'fit-in' to the PWI mainstream will never make us whole. We must learn the countless lessons of resistance to enslavement, and yes, suicide, that this White ideal of 'success' isn't the only way for us all to live. From my experience, and what this chapter and book have articulated, we must use the existing performative platforms of appeasement DEI as cover, a platform upon which to build towards true liberation. If they want more 'representation' (i.e. 'diversity') through 'cluster' hires, be sure to onboard those new hires with a fundamental understanding of the system that is meant to exploit and debase. If they only give you a month to celebrate in October or February, use that as a platform to spring grassroots mobilization and organization for yearlong activism and agitation. If they give you a seat at the table as a 'token,' be sure to put your foot in the door and allow more of you to come. At the bare minimum, recognize that knowledge is power, so be as transparent as possible to share what you've learnt (and heard) behind closed doors and share with the masses.

Conclusion: Towards a Radical Reorientation of Liberation

It may sound like Black nihilism, but on most days when I wake up, I'm reminded about the essentialist reduction of Black 'elitism' in academia through the words of Malcolm X (i.e. those with a PhD): 'What does a white man call a black man with a Ph.D.?' ... 'A nigger with a Ph.D' (Yancy, 2018, para. 1). If that is how the world sees me, if that is how my university sees me, with all my degrees and credentials, it is comforting to know that I am not a n****r, nor will I embody your oppression. I understand that this subaltern articulation is a violent reaction designed to hurt me mentally, physically, psychologically, and emotionally. My counterstrike exists in my full humanity, and unapologetically, as a Black academic.

This chapter has argued that emancipation cannot be achieved through frameworks designed to pacify. Diversity, equity, and inclusion (DEI), when stripped of any premise of structural transformation, becomes an instrument of appeasement rather than liberation. History teaches us that freedom has never been gifted; it has been seized through struggle, often under conditions of violence. By reframing violence beyond physical confrontation to include psychological, epistemic, and ideological disruption, we reclaim its role as a catalyst for change. From Fanon's insistence on decolonization as a total rupture, to Mandela's strategic embrace of sabotage, to Hampton's call for revolution as healing, the lesson is clear: liberation demands confrontation with systems that thrive on our subjugation.

As we move towards the book's conclusion, we must ask: What does it mean to operationalize these insights in our present moment? How do we translate historical lessons and radical *praxis* into actionable strategies that dismantle White supremacy rather than decorate it? The final section synthesizes these threads – Black-first *praxis*, historical models of resistance, and the imperative to reject appeasement – and offers a roadmap for imagining and enacting futures where freedom is not a slogan but a lived reality.

References

Anderson, N. J. (1942). Guerrilla warfare. *Command and General Staff School Military Review*, *22*(84), 42–45.

Beckles, H. M. (2013). *Britain's Black debt: Reparations for Caribbean slavery and native genocide*. University of the West Indies Press.

DeGruy, J. (2017). *Post traumatic slave syndrome: America's legacy of enduring injury and healing* (Revised ed.). Joy DeGruy Publications.

Du Bois, W. E. B. (1903). The talented tenth. In B. T. Washington, W. E. B. Du Bois, P. L. Dunbar, & C. W. Chesnutt (Eds.), *The Negro problem* (pp. 31–75). AMS Press.

Fanon, F. (1963/2004). *The wretched of the Earth* (R. Philcox, Trans.). Grove Press.

Halloran, M. J. (2019). African American health and posttraumatic slave syndrome: A terror management theory account. *Journal of Black Studies*, *50*(1), 45–65. https://doi.org/10.1177/0021934718803737

Hampton, F. (1969). *Power anywhere where there's people*. Marxist Internet Archive. https://www.marxists.org/archive/hampton/1969/misc/power-anywhere-where-theres-people.htm

James, C. L. R. (1963). *The Black jacobins: Toussaint l'ouverture and the San Domingo revolution* (2nd ed.). Vintage Books.

King, M. L. Jr. (1959). The social organization of nonviolence. *Liberation*, *4*, 5–6. https://kinginstitute.stanford.edu/king-papers/documents/social-organization-nonviolence

King, M. L. Jr. (1963, April 16). *Letter from a Birmingham jail [Letter, reproduced]*. African Studies Center, University of Pennsylvania. https://www.africa.upenn.edu/Articles_Gen/Letter_Birmingham.html

Lodge, T. (2006). *Mandela: A critical life*. Oxford University Press.

Mandela, N. (1995). *Long walk to freedom: The autobiography of Nelson Mandela*. Back Bay Books.

Marshall, Y. G. (2019, August 18). *Re-shelve civil rights, we need something stronger today*. Al Jazeera. https://www.aljazeera.com/opinions/2019/8/18/re-shelve-civil-rights-we-need-something-stronger-today

Merriam-Webster. (n.d.). Emancipate. In *Merriam-Webster dictionary*. https://www.merriam-webster.com/dictionary/emancipate

Satzewich, V. (1991). *Racism and the incorporation of foreign labour: Farm labour migration to Canada since 1945*. Routledge.

Spivak, G. C. (1988). Can the subaltern speak? In C. Nelson & L. Grossberg (Eds.), *Marxism and the interpretation of culture* (pp. 271–313). University of Illinois Press.

Walcott, R. (2021). *On property: Policing, prisons, and the call for abolition*. Biblioasis.

Warren, C. L. (2015). Black nihilism and the politics of hope. *CR: The New Centennial Review*, *15*(1), 215–248.

West, C. (2016). *The radical King*. Penguin Random House.

Yancy, G. (2018, April 29). The ugly truth of being a black professor in America. *The Chronicle of Higher Education*, *64*(34). https://www.chronicle.com/article/the-ugly-truth-of-being-a-black-professor-in-america/

Chapter 10

Conclusion: Reframing DEI and Owning Your Racism

Reflections on the Book

This book began with a question: *What does it mean to live and work in a fundamentally anti-Black society while navigating the contradictions of DEI?* From the Negro-Apocalypse of 25 May 2020 to the sanitized corporate DEI responses, we have traced how these frameworks were never designed for liberation but for appeasement. Through historical analysis, personal narrative and practical frameworks, this book has shown that DEI cannot deliver systemic change without radical accountability and Black-centred strategies. My personal narrative, as the Black son of Bajan newcomers, was not anecdotal; it was the lens through which we examined DEI as both a livelihood and a contradiction throughout this book.

This book started by revisiting 25 May 2020, a moment that seemed to promise systemic change, but was centuries in the making. I asked you to pause and remember 25 May 2020, the day the quiet world of the global pandemic got loud; the day George Floyd's murder became the catalyst for what I have called the Negro-Apocalypse. That moment was not an isolated rupture; rather, it was centuries in the making, rooted in colonialism, enslavement and the appeasement politics of multiculturalism. This illusion was an illusion of progress. This book argued that DEI is not a radical departure from these systems, but their modern extension; a mechanism to pacify resistance while preserving power.

What I Set Out to Do in Writing This Book

My objective in this undertaking was clear: to unmask DEI as a system-preserving mechanism and propose Black-first *praxis* as a pathway to liberation. We promised to move beyond the optics of inclusion and towards

Unmasking DEI, 149–157

doi:10.1108/978-1-83708-356-520261010

structural transformation. Each chapter delivered on this promise: tracing history, critiquing policy and offering radical alternatives for the future.

Across these pages, several interconnected themes have emerged. We traced the genealogy of DEI from its origins in civil rights movements to its current iteration as corporate appeasement, revealing how a framework intended for justice has been diluted into optics and performance. We examined the contradictions of *post*-racism and the institutional laundering of Black rage; or, the ways systems simultaneously celebrate diversity while perpetuating structural harm. We explored cultural frameworks such as Afrofuturism, soca and Black-first *praxis*, which offer imaginative and practical pathways for liberation beyond assimilation. Finally, we confronted the historical erasure of Black presence in Canadian institutions and underscored the urgent need for reparative justice. Taken together, these threads remind us of a sobering truth: DEI was never designed for liberation. It was designed to manage dissent, pacify resistance and preserve the status quo.

Where Do We Go From Here? Starting With the Self

One critical aspect often missing from DEI discourse is the interrogation of Self. In 2020, many White people were asked – by Black people and some White 'allies' – to examine and unlearn their 'White privilege.' Some responded by writing books, profiting from the moment. While this call for self-examination was necessary and long overdue, it also sparked a global anti-woke backlash. White people were (rightfully) implicated in the structural inequalities embedded in Western society and were asked to reflect on how they arrived at their current positions – both professionally and personally.

This sparked widespread discomfort and resistance. And for the record, I believe that this initial wave of DEI engagement was a meaningful first step, albeit one that was met with swift and fierce opposition. Many White people countered with claims of having grown up poor or lacking any form of privilege. These conversations, whether in classrooms or boardrooms, often devolved into unproductive shouting matches; a veritable Oppression Olympics of who had less money, more student debt or tougher childhoods. What could have been a foundational dialogue about positional and institutional power dynamics became the first casualty of the anti-woke and anti-DEI agenda.

Yet, for those still working within the often sanitized world of corporate DEI – what I call the 'appeasement DEI' space – there remains a way forward. There is still a way to 'slip the broccoli into the casserole'. We can still engage in conversations about White privilege – without necessarily using the words 'White' or 'privilege'. One effective approach is to reframe the conversation through the lens of leadership, specifically what I have termed the *Four I's of Inclusive Leadership*: Introspection, Intention, Implementation and Integrity. I have spent years 'real world' testing this concept, not just in academic environments, but in corporations and everyday life. The Four I's of Inclusive Leadership are the culmination of my personal, academic and administrative experiences in the DEI world.

Introspection

> *Look in the mirror and list ten things about your Self. No one is listening. No one is watching. It is just you. Be honest.*

Introspection is the closest we come to revisiting the 'White privilege' discourse that gained traction in 2020. Think of it as a modern reframing of Peggy McIntosh's 1989 metaphor of the 'invisible knapsack', a tool used for decades to help people recognize the everyday advantages they may take for granted. Rather than discarding this concept, we can repackage it in a way that aligns with the language of corporate and institutional environments.

This reframing also challenges the binary of 'White versus Black' and instead explores 'White' versus 'Black' as ideological constructs. It acknowledges that power and privilege often operate in the grey margins where individuals, regardless of race, may adopt behaviours aligned with White supremacy for reasons ranging from survival to social mobility in predominantly White spaces.

Introspection invites individuals to see themselves not through the lens of race, gender or settler identity, but simply as people. One exercise I use is deceptively simple: I ask participants to go home, look in the mirror, and write down 10 honest things about themselves. No one else will see the list; it's just them, their thoughts and their insecurities. The goal is not judgement, but self-awareness.

To avoid triggering defensiveness or guilt – especially among White participants – I encourage a shift in vocabulary. Instead of focusing on 'privilege' or 'power', I ask them to consider the concept of comfort. Here's the exercise:

- When you wake up in the morning, do you feel discomfort?
- When deciding how to style your hair, do you feel discomfort?
- When choosing what to wear, do you feel discomfort?
- When walking to your car at night, do you feel discomfort?
- When answering 'How was your weekend?' at work, do you feel discomfort?

If the answer is consistently 'no', then it is likely that society has been structured to accommodate your comfort. This is, in essence, a conversation about privilege, but framed in a way that invites reflection rather than resistance.

This reframing also opens the door to intersectionality. It allows people to recognize that comfort and discomfort are not solely determined by race. A White man may feel comfortable in some spaces but uncomfortable in others due to class, sexuality or disability. A Black woman may feel discomfort due to race and gender, but comfort in other aspects of her identity. This approach encourages people to ask: Why do I feel comfortable here? Why do I feel discomfort there? For example, a man may feel comfortable walking alone at night because he doesn't fear sexual assault. That's not just male privilege, it's a window into broader conversations about patriarchy, gender-based violence and societal expectations. By shifting the focus from identity labels to lived experiences of comfort and discomfort, we create a space where people are more likely to listen, engage and reflect.

Ultimately, introspection is a conversation about individual and institutional power, as well as how those forces intersect to benefit those already in positions of advantage. By reframing the conversation in this way, we can move beyond blame and shame, and instead foster a culture of honest reflection, shared responsibility and inclusive leadership.

Intention

> *This is the easy one; the 'talk-the-talk' phase.*

It's the part where people spend hours in workshops and DEI training sessions, immersed in the book-learning version of activism. And while I may sound dismissive, these activities do have their place. If we examine models of allyship, we see a necessary intersection of three elements: emotional desire for change, knowledge and action. Without all three, the structure collapses.

Knowledge and action without emotional investment create a predatory space, often found in the ivory tower, where 'culture vultures' capitalize on DEI moments for personal or professional gain. On the other hand, emotion and action without knowledge create a wildfire – passionate but unfocused, exhausting people without producing meaningful change. That's why intention matters; it's the grounding force that ensures our actions are informed, strategic and sustainable.

There is value in books. There is value in classrooms, however you define them. A baseline understanding of terminology, history and contemporary realities is essential. Scrolling through TikTok or Instagram can be informative, but it cannot be the sole source of your DEI education. Policies are important – they provide structure and accountability – but as the saying goes, culture eats policy for breakfast. To change culture, you must understand its historical, sociological and political roots.

Intention is about recognizing that the answers are often already out there. People have asked these questions before. They've tested solutions. We don't need to reinvent the wheel; we need to read the manual, understand the terrain and then drive forward with purpose.

Implementation

> *This is where the rubber meets the road. You've talked the talk, now can you walk the walk?*

Implementation is where I see the greatest tension between actionable DEI and appeasement DEI. Many individuals and organizations are comfortable identifying problems. They're comfortable writing reports, issuing statements and drafting recommendations. But when it comes time to act, to implement those recommendations, this is where the 'yes, but...' and 'what-about-isms' begin.

It's like New Year's resolutions about fitness. On January 1st, gyms are packed. People buy the right clothes, hire trainers and set goals. For a few weeks, they're committed. They meal prep, count calories and feel good. But by February, the momentum fades. Life gets in the way. And they realize that staying fit requires the same effort and consistency that got them there in the first place.

Appeasement DEI is like buying the gym membership and never going. You can't claim to be fit if you don't do the work. And not just the visible work – the sweating and lifting – but the unseen work: the cooking, the discipline, the sacrifices. The removal of things that bring comfort but hinder progress.

That's what real DEI implementation requires: a fundamental shift in systems. Not just changing your outfit, but changing your lifestyle. It's hard, it's uncomfortable and it will change you. But that's the point. If you're not willing to be transformed, then you're not really doing the work.

Integrity

> *And now we return to where we began. Integrity is the thread that ties it all together.*

I once had a conversation about inclusive hiring. One common practice is to assemble a 'diverse' hiring panel to signal commitment to DEI. But here's the problem; why exhaust the one Black person in your organization by putting them on every panel as a symbol of inclusion? That's not equity. It's exploitation. It's performative. It's virtue signalling.

What if we were just honest? What if we told candidates: 'We don't prioritize DEI. We care about profits. We'll pay you X dollars for your labour'. It may be harsh, but at least it's honest. Adults can handle the truth. We know racism exists. We know capitalism is exploitative. We know Santa Claus isn't real. Don't gaslight us with a fantasy of inclusion that doesn't exist.

If you're racist, own it. I'm not saying double down on it, I'm saying stop hiding it behind appeasement DEI. Because when you suppress it, it manifests in more insidious ways. It shows up in microaggressions, in tokenism, in the slow erosion of trust. And then the people most harmed are expected to be grateful for the crumbs of 'progress'.

Integrity means having the courage to interrogate your own motivations, to ask: What am I trying to protect? What am I trying to maintain? Are you co-opting the language of the oppressed to undermine their progress? Are you playing the role of the 21st-century orientalist, entering communities not to support, but to destabilize from within?

Moving Towards Institutional Change: Recommendations for Leaders and Policymakers

The shifts necessary in how we understand ourselves and our roles in the context of DEI are virtually meaningless without intentioned and sustainable changes to institutional policy and practice. The changes that I recommend here are rooted in the ethos established throughout this book, built on the theorizing and voices of Black, Indigenous and racialized leaders across space and time, offering tangible strategies to address the failures of the existing DEI paradigm. Each of these strategies is based in the following principles:

- *Accountability* and *Transparency*, which ask institutions to publish and share the institutional machinations that are often obscured through the neoliberal, post-racial lens of the ivory towers. These machinations may include leadership effectiveness and compensation, equity efforts and progress (or lack thereof) and funding schemes.
- *Inclusive* and *Ethical Leadership*, which require leaders to own their own racism, as well as their institution's, rather than hide behind DEI and other performative measures that create an illusion of progress. The Four I's of Inclusive Leadership detailed above provides a strong framework to accomplish this principle.
- *Capacity Building* and *Resource Redistribution*, which involve institutional commitments to altering the existing distribution of resources, opportunities for advancement and funding. These alterations may come in the form of increased funding and purview for Black-led research, commitments to partnerships (and benefits) for communities and the revision of hiring and tenure practices towards more diverse scholarship and faculty.
- *Structural Change*, which includes fundamental shifts to the structure of institutional policy, governance and practice that would render appeasement DEI institutionally impossible. These shifts may include embedding anti-racism and intersectionality in the language and implementation of policy, re-evaluating existing policies in the context of equity and assuming an ethic of relational belonging, privileging mutual respect without assimilation.

The following policy shorts, drawn from the key gaps identified throughout this book and rooted in these principles, are actionable steps to change institutional policy, governance and practice.

Policy Short 1: Define DEI Beyond Performative Gestures

DEI is often reduced to symbolic representation and one-off training sessions, failing to address structural inequities. Instead, we must:

- *Clarify definitions*: Adopt institution-wide definitions of diversity, equity and inclusion that emphasize structural change, not tokenism.

- *Embed accountability in law and policy*: Align DEI mandates with legal frameworks and require annual audits.
- *Move beyond representation*: Shift focus from 'who is in the room' to who has power and voice.

Policy Short 2: Confront Institutional Silence

There can be no more 'silent years;' it is necessary to address the systemic gatekeeping reflected in the historical exclusion of Black faculty and students in PWIs (and in leadership roles in corporations). To interrupt the silence, we must:

- *Audit historical records*: Commission institutional histories to uncover patterns of exclusion.
- *Set representation benchmarks*: Establish measurable targets for hiring and retention of Black faculty and staff.
- *Governance reform*: Audit Senate and Board structures for anti-Black racism.

Policy Short 3: Pivot to Black-First Praxis

DEI frameworks often perpetuate assimilation into inequitable systems. Liberation, however, requires Black-first *praxis*. As such, we must:

- *Institutionalize Afrocentric knowledge*: Fund Black Studies and embed Black epistemologies in curricula.
- *Support cultural resistance*: Recognize cultural forms as legitimate sites of knowledge and liberation.
- *Challenge systemic design*: Apply systems-thinking to dismantle structures that perpetuate inequity.

Policy Short 4: Address Structural Violence and Cultural Trauma

Anti-Black racism operates within the ivory towers through systemic and psychological violence. Institutions have the responsibility to support those within their walls. Accordingly, we must:

- *Recognize race-based cultural trauma*: Integrate culturally competent mental health supports.
- *Normalize epistemic resistance*: Protect academic freedom for critical race and Black feminist scholarship.
- *Enable grassroots disruption*: Support decentralized, student-led equity initiatives.

Policy Short 5: Move Beyond **The Scarborough Charter***'s Limits*

Despite its proposed benefits for diversity, equity and inclusion, *The Scarborough Charter* risks becoming another appeasement tool if not implemented with structural accountability. To resist the move to appeasement, we must:

- *Reframe the concept of 'inclusive excellence'*: Replace Eurocentric metrics with community impact measures.
- *Audit governance bodies*: Require anti-settler colonial audits of Boards and Senates.
- *Adopt Sankofa principles*: Embed historical lessons of Black resistance into institutional strategies.

Policy Short 6: Reparations as Equity

True equity requires reparatory justice for historical and systemic harms caused by enslavement and colonization. Framing the work of Mariame Kaba and Shira Hassan's book, *Fumbling Towards Repair: A Workbook for Community Accountability Facilitators* (2019), to move *towards repair*, we must:

- *Institutional reparations*: Fund scholarships, research chairs and community partnerships for Black communities.
- *Adopt CARICOM's 10-Point Plan principles*: Include education reform, cultural institutions and psychological rehabilitation as key commitments.
- *Global solidarity*: Align institutional policies with UNDPAD objectives (Recognition, Justice, Development).

Policy Short 7: Barbados as a Model for Liberation

Barbados' liberation movements show that systemic change requires collective action and education reform. From their guidance, we must:

- *Reform education systems*: Audit curricula for colonial legacies and Eurocentric dominance.
- *Institutionalize 'shadow strategies'*: Embed equity infrastructure during DEI 'moments' to withstand backlash.
- *Support transnational Black solidarity*: Fund research and exchange programmes connecting local DEI efforts to global liberation.
- *Challenge edutocracy*: Legitimize Afrocentric knowledge systems in policy and accreditation standards.

Coming to an End, Moving to New Beginnings

This book has challenged conventional ways of engaging with DEI, the appeasement DEI that I sorely find to be ineffective and performative. Have I (re)introduced concept that may be familiar to some but foreign to others? Yes. Have I written about some of my 'secrets' that have allowed me to navigate this space to have the ability to even write this book? Yes. Have I dug deep into the archives of discomfort that may, or may not, make people feel uncomfortable about my unapologetic engagement with my Self, my Four Is and my Black-focused ways of being? Yes. At the end of the day, it's about providing solutions that have worked for me, and for the generations of Black people before me. I am not here to reinvent the wheel, nor do I believe that these are the *only* solutions on how to survive and navigate oppressive structures. What I am saying is that we need to look back to go forward. We need to learn from those that came before us. We need to see the reality around us. We need to understand that the Negro-Apocalypse of the 2020s was 8 minutes of 46 seconds of centuries of oppression and violence. We need to understand that the playing field is not fair, and we can't continue to play by *their* rules. We need to play by *ours*.

If you're not about this life, that's okay. Just say so. But have the ethical mindset to support a model of relational belonging. A 'two-row wampum' approach where we walk side by side, in mutual respect, without trying to assimilate or dominate. That's integrity. That's leadership. And that's the future of DEI, if we're willing to do the work.

Index